The Curtiss D-12 Aero Engine

Curtiss D-12-E engine, 435 hp, 1930. (Smithsonian photo A-4593.)

SMITHSONIAN ANNALS OF FLIGHT • NUMBER 7

The Curtiss D-12 Aero Engine

by

Hugo T. Byttebier

SMITHSONIAN INSTITUTION PRESS

City of Washington

1972

UNITED STATES GOVERNMENT PRINTING OFFICE
WASHINGTON : 1972

For sale by the Superintendent of Documents, U.S. Government Printing Office
Washington, D.C. 20402 - Price 75 cents
Stock Number 4705-000ι

Acknowledgments

This history of the Curtiss D–12 engine is the result of research extending over several years. It has been made possible through assistance provided by many persons and organizations.

From its inception the project received the careful attentions of Mr. Robert B. Meyer, Jr., curator, aero propulsion division, National Air and Space Museum, Smithsonian Institution. Other contributors include the following:

Dr. Arthur Nutt, designer of the D–12 engine; Mr. Lee M. Pearson and Mr. Eric Collins of the Bureau of Naval Weapons; Mr. Royal Frey of the Air Force Museum at Wright-Patterson Air Force Base; General James Doolittle; Major G. E. A. Hallett; Mr. Roland Rohlfs; Mr. Erik Hildes-Heim; Mr. Harold Morehouse; Mr. George Page; Mr. Theodore Wright; Technical Sergeant Merle Olmsted; Mr. Steve Wittman; Mr. Alan Phillips; Mr. Paul Matt; Mr. Thomas Foxworth; the Curtiss-Wright and Pratt & Whitney companies; Lieutenant Colonel F. E. Rudston Fell, D.S.O., O.B.E., Wing Commander Norman Macmillan, and the Rolls-Royce and Fairey companies, of Great Britain; Mr. Antonio M. Biedma of Argentina; and General Edmundo Vaca Medrano, former aeronautical attaché at the Bolivian Embassy in Buenos Aires.

Special thanks are due Mr. William Lewis, who interviewed Charles B. Kirkham, and Mr. Paul E. Garber, historian emeritus, National Air and Space Museum, who reviewed the original manuscript.

Contents

Introduction

The date 28 September 1923 is an important one in the annals of aviation. On that day, at Cowes in England, the sixth international race for the Schneider Cup was held, and on that day the Schneider race changed drastically from a contest to evaluate speed, reliability, and navigability of seaplanes to an all-out, high-speed competition between world powers.

This change was brought about by two sleek, diminutive Curtiss racers that had been brought from America to challenge the European seaplanes. The Curtiss planes ran away from their competitors so convincingly that even those who had foreseen the result were surprised at the extent of the victory. The apparent ease of the American win was forcefully significant, and the observant press was quick to praise the excellent combination of flying skill and advanced technology. The most important element of the victory soon was pinned down to the Curtiss D–12 engines. They proved to be powerful, light, and reliable, and they introduced a new dimension in power plants by having a frontal area for which one commentator found the correct adjective—"piccolissimo."

The D–12 engine is an excellent example of a first-line design in the history of aero engine development. It was the result not only of brilliant inspiration but of patient application, perseverance, and hard work on the part of its developers.

To understand the origins of the D–12 it is necessary to go back to the autumn of 1915. World War I was about to enter its second year, and to everyone concerned with aeronautics it had become obvious that the Germans had taken a lead in aero engine development. The quickly rising importance of the air arm caused the Allies to become increasingly aware of their shortage of adequate engines, especially of high-power units that would be decisive in the battle for aerial supremacy.

Several American engineering firms tried to develop aero engines that would be acceptable to the Allied flying services, but only a few were able to secure orders. The inherent problems of aircraft engine devel-

1

opment were made more acute by wartime difficulties. The fighting forces were continually exerting pressure on the technical limitations of an already highly sophisticated piece of machinery, thus imposing an unrelenting stress on designers and manufacturers.

One of the greatest efforts by an American firm toward the achievement of a first-class, high-power aero engine was undertaken by the Wright Aeronautical Corporation, successor to the original Wright Company. Wright Aeronautical, whose directors had seen the great future that lay in engine manufacture, already had gained control of the Simplex Automobile Company; and it had acquired the services of that firm's chief engineer, Henry M. Crane, who had built up quite a reputation because of the excellence of his Crane-Simplex motor cars.

In making the decision to embark upon the manufacture of high-power aero engines, the executives of Wright Aeronautical were aware that no quick results would be reached by starting on the design of yet another type of engine. Rather, they believed that the quickest and safest way to achieve big production potential was to build an engine based upon the most promising design being evolved in Europe. Thus, the firm sent Crane and another representative to France to evaluate the different types of aero engines being developed there and to determine the design best suited for production in the United States.

The story of the D–12 engine starts in the fall of 1915 with the arrival of the Wright mission in France. At that time a novel type of aero engine was passing through its tests with fair results. It had been built according to the ideas of Marc Birkigt, a young Swiss engineer. Some ten years earlier Birkigt had linked his talent to capital from Spain to enable that country to compete in the field of automobile manufacture. In this he had succeeded brilliantly, with the trade name Hispano-Suiza having become well known in the automotive world.

At the start of World War I, Birkigt had begun building an aviation engine along original ideas evolving from his company's successful automobile racing engines. When Wright's representatives arrived this aero engine was passing through a period of intense development prior to its being launched on large-scale production.

The usual water-cooled engine at that time consisted mainly of a very stiff and relatively heavy crankcase upon which steel cylinders were bolted individually. Each cylinder was surrounded by its own cooling mantle, while the valve mechanism in the head was, in most cases, left totally exposed. Birkigt's Hispano-Suiza engine departed radically from that type of construction. Its cylinders were formed from an aluminum, single-block casting into which were screwed four forged steel barrels

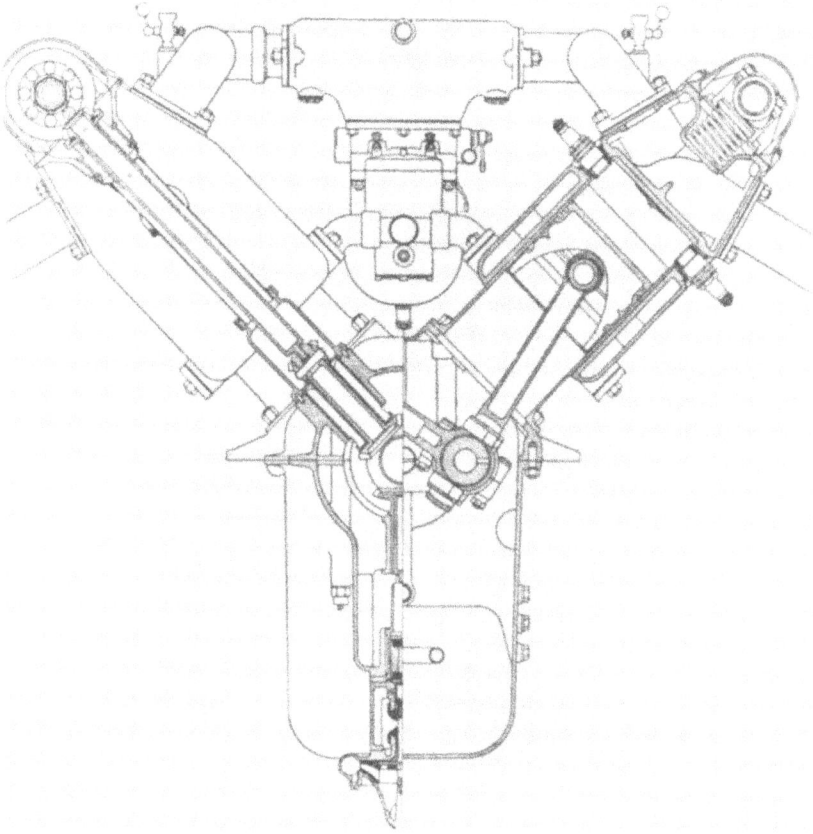

FIGURE 1.—Cross-sectional arrangement, Hispano-Suiza, 200 hp, of World War I. (Smithsonian photo A-53098.)

that were threaded on the outside for their entire length (Figures 1, 2). These barrels were closed at the top, forming a compartment that served as a combustion chamber. Because the barrels were screwed into the aluminum blocks, the passages for the cooling water were cored from the block; as a result, the heat imparted by the combustion process to the cylinder barrel had to pass through a part of the aluminum casting before it was affected by the cooling medium. This was one of the disadvantages of the design.

A very light crankcase was attached to the cylinder blocks; thus, the Hispano could be described as having the crankcase hung on the cylinders instead of having the cylinders on the crankcase. The valves, two per cylinder and mounted vertically in the cylinder head, were actuated

3

FIGURE 2.—Hispano-Suiza, Type I, 150 hp. (Smithsonian photo A-4593B.)

by a single overhead camshaft which operated the valve stems directly, without the interposition of either pushrods or rockers. The entire valve mechanism was enclosed in an oiltight cover that fitted closely over the cylinder block. The overall design resulted in a compact, clean, light, and apparently simple unit which inevitably attracted the attention and admiration of the engineering world.

The most outstanding feature of the Hispano-Suiza, however, was not the novelty of its design but its operating efficiency, something that hardly could be said of other designs, advanced or not, which many inspired and enthusiastic inventors were trying to adapt for use in airplanes. The Hispano's clean lines and reliability in operation derived more from its designer's outstanding talents in precision engineering than from any simplicity of design—a fact which several engine manufacturers, deluded into trying to improve upon the type, would soon discover.

By 1915 the Hispano-Suiza V-8 engine was developing 150 bhp at 1,450 rpm, and, thanks to Birkigt's long experience with precision

4

FIGURE 3.—Charles B. Kirkham
(1882-1969).

machine tools, it was ready for large-scale manufacture.

Henry Crane, through his appreciation of good engineering practice, recognized the Hispano-Suiza's superior design and great potential. Arrangements were made immediately between Wright Aeronautical and the French and Spanish parties involved for the granting of a license for manufacture in the United States. At the same time, an order for 450 engines was secured from the French government.

While these activities were in progress, developments also were taking place at the Curtiss firm, at that time the largest and oldest manufacturer of aero engines in the United States. In 1915 the company had secured the services of Charles B. Kirkham, a young engineer of great talent and long an acquaintance of Glen Curtiss. Kirkham, a builder of motorcycle engines since the the turn of the century, had built his first aero engine in 1910. He started his assignment as chief motor engineer at Curtiss by improving the existing OX and VX models, of 90 and 160 hp respectively (Figures 5, 6). The OX–5, destined for a long and famous career, already had been the object of important production orders from the Allied air services.

5

FIGURE 4.–John North Willys (1873-1935). (Photo courtesy of Automotive Old Timers, Inc.)

With an eye on developments in Europe, Curtiss, together with several other American engine builders, began, toward the end of 1915, a design study for the construction of a big aero engine of 300 or more horsepower. The quickest way to achieve this was thought at the Curtiss Company to be through enlarging the 8-cylinder VX model into a 12-cylinder engine. The first 12-cylinder Curtiss, designated the V–4, was, like the products of the other American manufacturers of big engines, of great weight and bulk (Figure 7); in fact, no such design had weighed under 1,000 lb, and the Curtiss V–4, when finished, turned the scales at nearly 1,100 lb, dry. Although the engine eventually developed about 400 bhp, it was not produced because a successful rival called the Liberty was lighter and had the same horsepower. In addition, Kirkham became interested in an entirely new design. The sole example of the V–4 ended as the power plant of a speedboat, *Miss Miami*.

The sudden appearance, in 1916, of the Wright Corporation as an engine manufacturer—introducing the 150-hp Hispano-Suiza in the United States with the avowed intention of mass-producing it—was

6

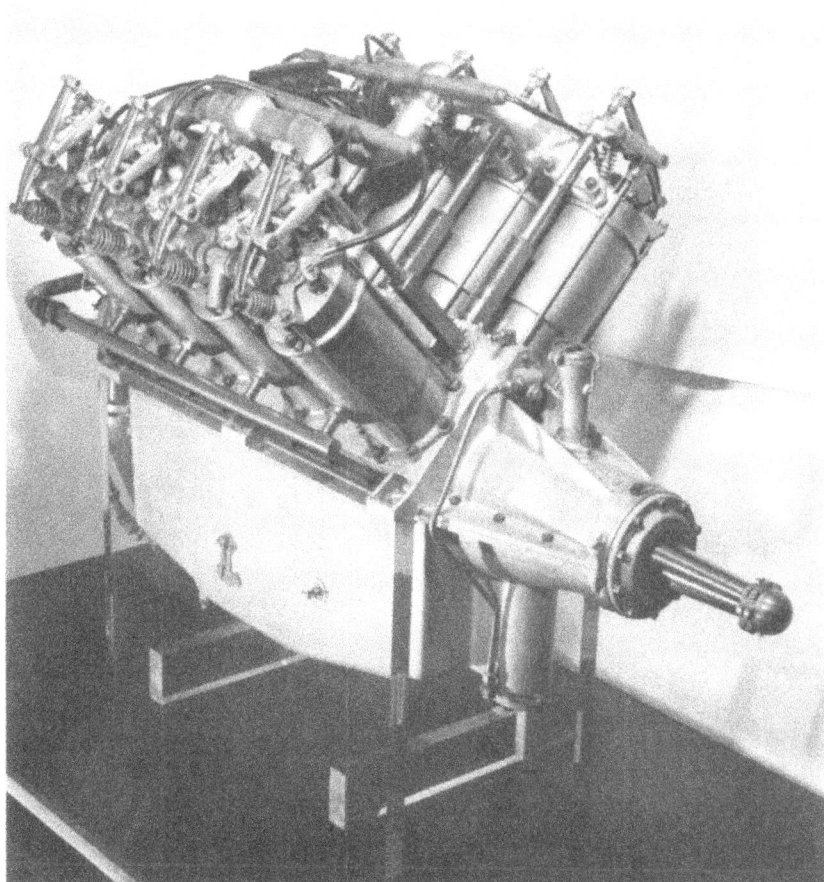

FIGURE 5.—Curtiss OX-5, 90 hp, World War I. United States National Air and Space Museum (NASM) specimen number 1920-8. (Smithsonian photo A-1832.)

viewed by the Curtiss management as a challenge, especially by John North Willys, Curtiss's energetic president and financial backer. No one seemed to doubt the Wright Corporation's ability to achieve what it had set out to do, and Willys feared that Curtiss's engine department, hitherto leading in the United States, was about to face strong competition. He also knew the Hispano's reputation, and he saw that Curtiss's unwieldy V-type engines would never be able to answer Wright's challenge. He instructed Kirkham to design an engine to compete with the Hispano-Suiza; and Kirkham, whose engineer's imagination was as much stirred by the high efficiency of monoblock construction as had

7

FIGURE 6.—Curtiss V-X, 160 hp, 1916. NASM number 1949-21.
(Smithsonian photo A-38654.)

been Crane's, decided that the only way to counter the threat from the Hispano was to build something better.

From Europe news had come that the Hispano-Suiza, by having a reduction gear fitted and its revolutions raised, was developing over 200 bhp. So Kirkham, very judiciously calculating the future needs of fighter aircraft as around 300 hp, determined, probably with full approval of the Curtiss management, to produce the world's foremost fighter engine. Thus, his first venture into high-speed engine manufacture was to be a 300-hp unit of small dimensions that would outperform the Hispano in every way.

8

FIGURE 7.—Curtiss V-4, 400 hp, 1917. NASM 1950-97. (Smithsonian photo A-4989.)

The new engine was to have twelve cylinders. At that time this was most unusual, especially for engines of fighter planes, as it was believed that the engine should be as short as possible so as not to impair the aerobatic properties of pursuit planes, then being driven by compact rotary engines. But Kirkham was after speed, and a 12-cylinder V-type engine would permit a much smaller frontal area than would a radial configuration or even a V-8, like the Hispano.

In his efforts to create an engine that would surpass the Hispano, Kirkham used the Hispano's progressive features only as basic inspiration for an engine so audaciously designed that even Birkigt's revolutionary project would appear conservative in comparison. Kirkham's first aluminum monoblock engine was known, in Curtiss nomenclature, as the model AB (Figure 8). It had a detachable cast-aluminum cylinder head into which six individual closed-end cylinder barrels, or sleeves, were screwed and heat-shrunk at the top only. The single aluminum casting included crankcase and water jackets, on top of which was bolted the cylinder head casting containing the sleeves. The steel sleeves were made to fit neatly inside their jackets without actual contact. A packing ring, fitted under heavy pressure at the lower end, sealed the cooling water in the jackets from the crankcase.

9

FIGURE 8.—Curtiss AB, 300 hp, 1916. (Smithsonian photo A-5235.)

Thus, by a masterful stroke, Kirkham had avoided the disadvantages of the "dry-sleeve" construction as found in the Hispano. In his engine, the cooling water was in direct contact with the barrel for nearly its entire length. This "wet-sleeve" construction was easy to obtain with individual cylinders as on the Mercedes or Liberty designs, which have their own cooling mantles neatly welded around them, but in the case of a monoblock engine it constituted a technical *tour de force*. The AB (and the later K–12) construction was to become the hallmark for all subsequent high-power design. It is interesting that Hispano-Suiza engineers eventually switched over to wet-sleeve construction, but not until 1928.

As it originally was proposed to have the AB run at very high crankshaft speeds, a reduction gear was embodied in the design. The housing of the gears even formed a part of the large crankcase and water-jacket casting, making the design even more complicated.

For improved breathing at high crankshaft speeds the AB had four valves per cylinder, against the Hispano's two. The valves were actuated by a single overhead camshaft through T-shaped cam followers, one follower operating the intake valves and the other the exhaust valves. The drive of the camshaft was at the center of each cylinder block, an arrangement that diminished the torsion problems but made the engine slightly longer. As in the Hispano, the valve mechanism was entirely enclosed in an oiltight cover and continuously lubricated.

The crankshaft, supported by four main bearings, was balanced only statically, with counterweights. The reduction gear pinion on the front end of the crankshaft had no outboard bearing because the design of the propeller shaft and its gear did not allow sufficient propeller clearance.

As compared to the 8-cylinder Hispano, Kirkham's AB had a smaller (4-in.) bore for a smaller frontal area, and a 5½-in. stroke for improved volumetric efficiency.

By the time the AB was ready for testing, April 1917 had arrived and the United States had entered World War I. The engine developed 300 bhp at 2,250 rpm but it saw very little test running for several reasons. Kirkham found that it was too heavy (at 725 lb) for the power developed. Then the gearing arrangement gave trouble, a portent of much that was to come. The valve-actuating mechanism was not satisfactory either, but still worse, in Kirkham's view, was the news that Hispano-Suiza was building an improved V-8 engine of 300 hp, also to be manufactured by Wright—which in the meantime had become Wright-Martin. So, Kirkham scrapped the AB and proceeded without delay on a new design.

Kirkham's new engine, first known as the D–1200 (Figure 9) had a half inch greater bore and stroke (4½ by 6 in.) than the AB, displaced 1,145 cubic inches against the new Hispano's 1,127, and was intended to furnish 400 bhp and run at an unheard-of 2,500 rpm—all this with a designed weight of only 625 lb.

From today's viewpoint, one wonders at the daring and foresight of Kirkham, who brought out a fighter engine of 400 bhp at a time when a proposed United States Standard Engine (known as the Liberty), believed to cover all existing needs, was planned as a V-8 of between 250 and 275 hp. The fact that the big new Hispano-Suiza eventually materialized as a direct-drive, slower turning (1,800 rpm) engine did not impress Kirkham; or, if it did, he paid no heed, for so possessed had he now become by his inspiration that he no longer was to be deterred by technical difficulties or problems with metallurgy.

The greatest improvement over the AB was in the flow of the exhaust gases. In the D–1200 the valves were actuated by two camshafts, one for the exhaust and one for the inlet valves. Consequently, all exhaust valves could be located on the outside of each cylinder block, where they opened into individual ports for unhampered escape of burnt gases. The exhaust ports fitted into a big collector which ejected the gases

FIGURE 9.—Curtiss D-1200, 400 hp, 1917. (Photo courtesy of U.S. Air Force Museum. Smithsonian photo A-4618A.)

directly upward through a large central chimney at each side of the engine. Carburetion was by a new Ball and Ball Duplex type DVA–3, and the two magnetos were Ericsson-Berling model D–66 X–4. Each magneto fired one bank of cylinders, but this procedure was not well thought out—a magneto failure resulted in an immediate loss of half the engine power. The A.C. spark plugs were all located on the inside of the V formed by the two banks of cylinders. As in the AB model, the crankshaft was supported by four main bearings, but there was an added fifth outboard bearing in front of the reduction gear for extra support.

Inaugurating a new breakthrough in aero engine technology, a mechanically driven, partly built-in supercharger was to be installed at the rear of the new engine. It was to be driven by a long shaft running through the center of the V and to be geared to the reduction gear at the

FIGURE 10.—Curtiss K-6, 150 hp, 1919. (Smithsonian photo A-4991A.)

front of the engine. A friction clutch was inserted near the front end of the driving shaft to eliminate all possibility of any torsional or accelerating forces being transmitted to the supercharger impeller. Four mechanically driven superchargers built by General Electric were ordered in 1917. Two of these were requisitioned by McCook Field's engineering division, at that time busy with development of the exhaust-driven turbosupercharger for the Liberty engine. The other two units were delivered to the Curtiss Company, but development work on the superchargers lagged because the engine itself demanded every possible effort from Kirkham and his team. Later, the supercharger was found to be unsatisfactory, but the idea for its use was significant in that it showed Kirkham's early preoccupation with a feature that would come into use a full ten years later.

FIGURE 11.—Curtiss K-12, 375 hp, 1918. (Photo courtesy of U.S. Air Force Museum. Smithsonian photo A-4618.)

The new engine soon became truly identified with Kirkham by its official designation, the K–12; and usually it was referred to as the Kirkham or Curtiss-Kirkham engine. The prototype K–12 was bench-tested (in the last week of 1917) at a weight of 625 lb, as designed. A six-cylinder unit, the K–6 (Figure 10), was developed along parallel lines. It really was half a K–12 (without reduction gears and other pretentions toward high power) that was rated at 150 hp at 1,700 rpm.

Undoubtedly, Kirkham had become fully aware that his K–12 (Figures 11, 12), with its very small frontal area and high power, stood unchal-

14

FIGURE 12.—Curtiss K-12, 1918. (Smithsonian photo A-4594A.)

lenged; and, afraid lest his brainchild be wasted on some cumbersome or indifferent airplane, he undertook at once to design a fighter that would be able to use the K–12 to its best account— a battle plane that would outperform any existing airplane as completely as he believed the K–12 would eclipse every existing engine. Here was a case of a single designer being able to devote his talents not only to developing a new, untried engine but also to designing a new airplane that would utilize it.

The new airplane had characteristics that were extremely progressive and original, following the true Kirkham touch. Full advantage was taken of the low frontal area of the K–12, with the fuselage closely tailored around the engine. This was a new departure in design, as hitherto the engines somehow had been fixed onto the airplanes. A possible exception was the French SPAD, which was built to take full advantage of the compactness of the Hispano-Suiza, and it may have inspired Kirkham to some extent. Pure speed had not been uppermost in the minds of aircraft designers up to that time, as so many other qualities had to be considered. The trend toward the combining of a small, powerful engine with a wholly streamlined aircraft for obtaining higher speeds had started, however, in 1917.

Kirkham's airplane is described in the first edition of the *Aircraft Yearbook* (1919, page 121): "The craft is a triumph in streamlining. Not a square inch of the machine, from tail skid to exhaust pipes, has been omitted from the careful plan of shaping, which has cut resistance to the minimum."

With high speed now secured by high power, complete streamlining, and a small engine, Kirkham proceeded to expand on the theme by using three wings on the plane's fuselage. Kirkham believed that a triplane would increase maneuverability and climbing capability. To top it all, the fighter was to be a two-seater, with the pilot having two synchronized guns at his command and with the gunner, in the rear, having two movable guns, thus adding maximum firepower to highest speed and optimum climbing ability. This promised to become by far the most formidable airplane designed since the beginning of the war, and more than others it deserved the name of "battleplane" that was applied to it.

Capitalizing on the big promise of the K–12 and the triplane, Willys approached the United States Navy and pressed for a big contract as soon as possible. In spite of entreaties from the developers of the geared Liberty, then on test, that that engine was more suited for its needs, the Navy did not have the fixed idea for "one standard engine in one standard plane." On 30 March 1918 the Navy placed an order with Curtiss for two triplanes and four K–12 engines.

On 5 July 1918 the K–12 went up for the first time, powering the triplane on its maiden flight. Roland Rohlfs, Curtiss test pilot, was at the controls, and his take-off was significantly short.

Progress of both airplane and engine was watched with keen interest. In the first flights the four-blade propeller braked the engine at 1,900 rpm, restraining power and speed, so a new two-blade propeller was fitted. The side radiators cooled too much, so smaller ones were installed; but then the engine overheated on the fast climbing tests. The problem was solved by adapting a by-pass device that eliminated use of part of the larger radiator during horizontal flight.

It was clear from the first flights that the triplane stood up magnificently to its claim for speed and climb; and it already had shown itself capable of outdistancing a DH-4 with ease. Rohlfs claimed that the climb was in the neighborhood of 2,000 ft/min, and maximum speed was assumed to be around 150 mph. Both figures represented performances greater than any other airplane had been known to achieve.

The first official flight finally was made on 19 August, and trials were held from 1 September to 5 September. The witnessing Navy officers, Holden C. Richardson and C. N. Liqued, may hardly have believed the figures when it was shown that the 18–T—as the triplane was now designated—on its first official flight had reached a best speed, over a measured course, of 162 mph in full military trim. The previous officially recognized speed record had been set at 126 mph, in September 1913.

The first triplane (Figures 13, 14) was given Bureau No. A–3325; the second was assigned the number A–3326. After the first official trials the Navy was willing to order 750 K–12 engines at once, but the Bureau of Aircraft Production decreed that this order was not to interfere with the priority of materials destined for the Liberty engine, the mass production of which already was underway. But to the great chagrin and disappointment of everyone concerned, including the naval officers delegated at the Curtiss plant to supervise manufacture, no large orders were placed.

The reasons for the Navy's reluctance were valid enough. The K–12 had not yet passed a 50-hour acceptance test; also, interest in triplanes was on the wane at that time. Allied authorities had stated that triplanes were not satisfactory, and certainly not for two-seat fighters, because of poor visibility and lack of stability as a gun platform. It was clear also that the war was nearing its end and the time for large contracts was past.

The Army had already approached Kirkham for a biplane version of the 18–T to be built along similar lines; and the Navy also had stated

FIGURE 13.–Curtiss-Kirkham 18-T Wasp triplane, about 1919, with Curtiss K-12 engine, 1918. (Smithsonian photo A-4597.)

a preference for a biplane—if possible, a seaplane—and after the September tests it had recommended conversion of the triplane into a seaplane. As a result, in the summer of 1919 the A–3325 was converted, using floats of the N–9 type, and it reached 126 mph during tests. In April 1920 this aircraft set a world's seaplane speed record at 138 mph. Later, both triplanes were prepared as racing landplanes, with the aft seat faired in.

The Army first had evinced interest when it had asked Curtiss to lend it the Navy's A–3325 for test flights. This plane was flown at Wilbur Wright Field on 18 September but it showed the same troubles with overheating, due to the smallness of the radiator, as it had on the earlier Navy tests. In the meantime, the Army's engineering division had written a report on the biplane design the Army had asked for. This report, based on the data given by the Curtiss Company and signed by Alexander Klemin, bears the date 13 August 1918 and the serial number 267.

Criticism was made of the single gun on the turret for the observer, though there was another gun on a flexible mount in the floor. When the time came to evaluate the K–12 engine, it was noted that 400 bhp was claimed at 2,350 rpm on a 6:1 compression ratio with a weight of

18

FIGURE 14.—The 18-T triplane with floats. (Smithsonian photo A-4597A.)

680 lb. The weight figures were stated as being "Much below present best practice. There either is an error in the weights or the motor may have to be carefully watched." The phrase "present best practice" meant, of course, the Liberty engine. It also was noted that the weight of the K–12, given as 625 lb in June 1918, had been raised to 660 lb and finally, in August, to 680 lb. Curtiss then was given Order CS–152, for two biplanes and two triplanes. One plane of each type was to be statically tested to ascertain the true limits of strength, while the others were to be thoroughly tested in flight. The static tests of the first triplane, delivered to McCook Field in February 1919, revealed serious weaknesses in several components. The first biplane was delivered in June 1919, after it had been displayed in New York at the Madison Square Garden show in March. It received number SC–40454 and became the P–86. Its crash, soon afterwards, ended the Army's interest in the type.

Meanwhile, the Wright-Martin Corporation had been experiencing difficulties in its efforts to bring the Hispano-Suiza to mass production. It was clear from the start that the design of that engine was not one that could be copied easily, and considerable delays were suffered for different reasons. To make things worse, new specifications for improved ratings were coming from France, raising the power first to

19

FIGURE 15.—Hispano-Suiza Type H, 300 hp, 1919. (Smithsonian photo A-4594B.)

180 hp, then to 200 hp, and later to 220 hp. It was not noted, however, that as horsepower ratings went up, reliability went down.

In the face of these conflicting interests, Wright decided, wisely, to stay with the original design and direct all efforts towards bringing the 150-hp model to production as soon as possible. But not much headway was made at first. The chief difficulties lay in the extreme stringency of the specifications for the different materials and in the excessively small tolerances to which every piece had to be finished, making the work more difficult than watchmaking. The famous cast-aluminum cylinder blocks were giving nightmares to all concerned, and most of the troubles were solved only when the company had established its own aluminum foundry, working at superior refinements. Production finally started at the beginning of 1918, but by then the proud "Hisso" fighter engine of 1916 had become suitable for trainer duties only.

When the blueprints for the new 300-hp model finally arrived, preparations were made promptly for its speedy production, but the solving

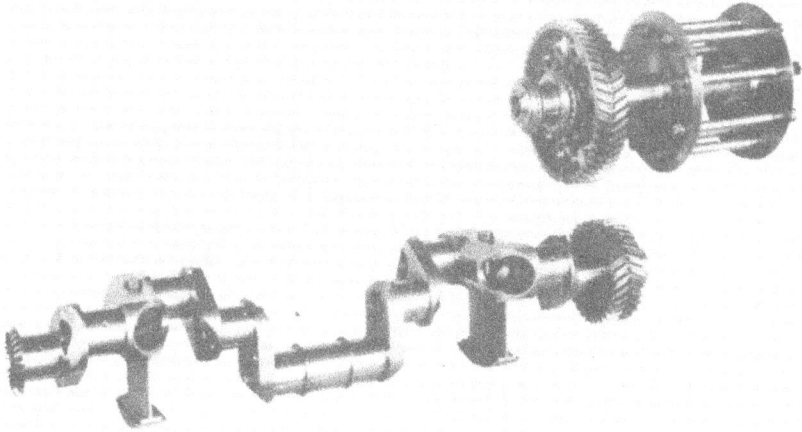

FIGURE 16.— Crankshaft and propeller shaft, showing reduction gears, of Curtiss K-12, 1919. (Smithsonian photo A-4594D.)

of problems similar to those with the smaller types resulted in the new model (Figure 15) not being ready for production until near the end of 1919. Still, the fact remains that the small Hispano finally was produced successfully in satisfactory numbers. Two British attempts to improve on the Hispano form of construction—the Siddeley Puma and the Sunbeam Arab—had not been successful, and subcontractors were running into trouble everywhere. (The fitting of steel cylinder liners in aluminum blocks still is considered a major problem by automobile manufacturers today.)

Against this background it is easier to understand why the K–12, which was intended to outperform the Hispano in many ways, encountered numerous difficulties. The main troubles were related to the reduction gear, the large aluminum casting, and the crankshaft (Figure 16).

The reduction gear troubles were particularly irritating because they were a necessary evil. The problem basically stemmed from the opposing relationships between the engine, which, in becoming lighter and smaller, could run faster, and the propeller, which gained in efficiency by running slower. In the case of the propeller, the rotational speed was further limited by enormous problems that arose when the velocity of the tips reached the speed of sound. This put an upper limit to propeller speed at about 2,000 rpm. A prudent safe maximum being considered at the time was around 1,800 rpm. The only solution lay—and still lies—in the provision of a form of gearing which reduces

21

the speed of the propeller shaft of the engine to a figure better suited to propeller efficiency. The problem is as old as aviation itself. The Wright brothers used, from the first, a crude but efficient form of gearing with bicycle chains.

The Hispano-Suiza was readily adaptable to high-speed running. The original model of 150 hp had been enabled to turn out increasing power ratings by the simple expedient of making the engine run faster. With crankshaft speeds of up to 2,150 rpm coming into use, the introduction of a reduction gearing became imperative. But at the same time it was found that the gearing was a delicate and tricky affair, and seizures were frequent. The big, 300-hp Hispano had been conceived in geared and ungeared form, but the geared form was not followed up and the crankshaft speed of the direct-drive production model was kept down to 1,800 rpm.

The K–12, which from the onset was designed for highest power and smallest size, could not dispense with the gears, which had a reduction ration of 5:3 (or 0.6), but here, too, continuous trouble-free running could not be attained in spite of the addition of a fifth bearing in front for the support of the pinion.

The integral construction of crankcase and water jackets in one aluminum casting, while making for great saving in weight and theoretical rigidity, really was a type of construction that bordered on the impossible. The blocks were cast at the Buffalo foundry of the Aluminum Company of America, which worked diligently and conscientiously to produce good castings, but such a complicated and large casting was beyond the art of the time. The results: too many blocks condemned because of warping, too many misruns, and too much porosity, doubtless due to the high pouring temperatures used in the attempt to avoid misruns.

The crankshaft, supported on four bearings and with counterweights for static balance only, was not reliable and breaking occurred easily. The situation could not be improved, and an exasperated Kirkham ended his attempts by refusing to strengthen the design and preferring to blame the material as faulty.

The first of six attempts to run an endurance test as required by the armed services was started at the Buffalo plant of the Curtiss Corporation on 9 August 1918 using K–12 engines 7, 8, and 9. The normal schedule to which any engine had to be submitted consisted of ten separate five-hour runs. The first half hour of each run was at full throttle and rated power, while the remaining four and a half hours were at 90 percent of rated power. Engines 7 and 8 weighed 665 lb, dry; engine 9 had a 24-lb counterweight added in the center of the crankshaft, raising its dry weight to 689 lb.

Test 1, with engine 8, was discontinued after 1 hour 36 minutes, full-throttle, when connecting-rod bearing 2 burned out because of breakage of the oil manifold.

Test 2, with engine 7, ended after 20 minutes of the third five-hour period (i.e., after 10 hours 20 minutes) when six teeth of the reduction gear on the crankshaft broke.

Test 3, with engine 8 after its oil manifold had been repaired and strengthened, was discontinued after only 4 minutes running when cylinders 1, 3, and 5 ceased firing. The breakdown occurred when parts of an auxiliary air valve of the front carburetor were sucked into the cylinders, holding the valves open and bending the valve stems. The auxiliary air valve was then redesigned.

Test 4 was the third attempt with engine 8, after it had been put in condition again. This time the K–12 ran well and hopes soared, but after 21 minutes of the third five-hour period the articulating boss on master connecting-rod 6 broke; as a result, the crankcase cracked between cylinders 5 and 7 and the base of cylinder 5 was damaged. This test marked the end of engine 8. The boss on master rods was strengthened on the other engines.

Test 5, with engine 7, was an all-out effort to make the 50 hours, but it was marred by numerous interruptions. The first stoppage came after 10 minutes running when the tachometer drive housing broke. It also was discovered that one camshaft bearing had broken. Heavier bearings were installed and the test was resumed, but after 5 minutes more there was a second interruption—the right-hand magneto drive shaft had frozen to the bushing in the tachometer drive gear housing. When this trouble was cured the engine went well for the remainder of the first five-hour period. After 20 minutes at full throttle in the second period there was another interruption when the clamping bolt of connecting-rod 2 broke away. The bolts were replaced with others having thicker heads. A fourth interruption, after 3 hours 8 minutes, was caused by the breaking of the lock screw for the tappet of the rear intake valve of cylinder 11, letting the valve drop into the cylinder. This lock screw had been bent in tightening. Lock washers were fitted and the test was resumed. After half an hour at full throttle and 4 hours 37 minutes at 90 percent power, the fifth interruption occurred when the oil line to the pressure gage at the crankcase cracked. After another 4 hours 9 minutes running, this test was at last discontinued when a lock nut on the rear of the propeller shaft broke. This time the engine

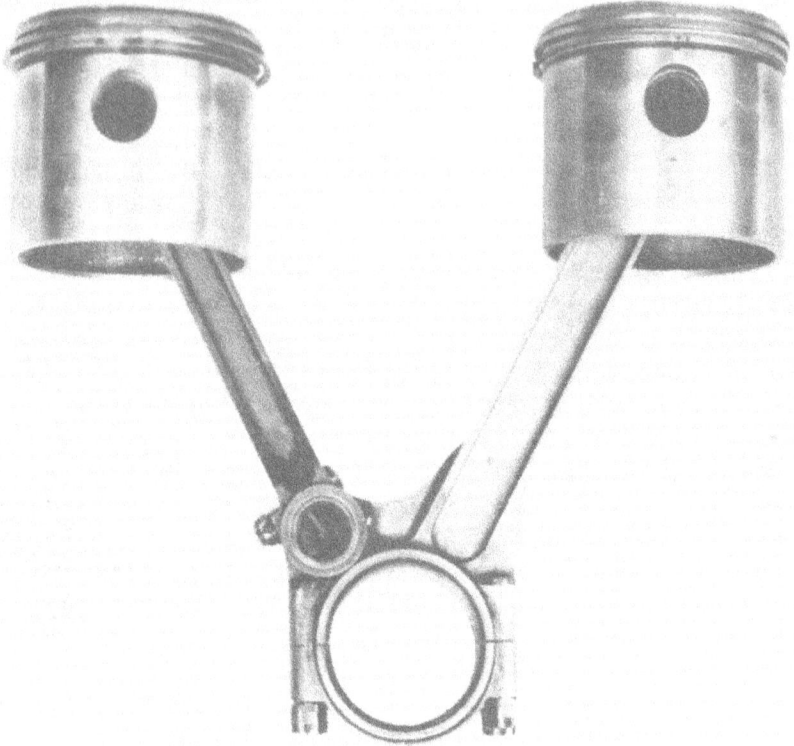

FIGURE 17.—Assembly of pistons and connecting rods, Curtiss K-12, 1919.

was ruined beyond repair because the propeller shaft shifted out. As the reduction gears on the propeller shaft and crankshaft were of the herringbone type, the propeller shaft pulled the crankshaft with it. This broke the oil feed line to the bearing and interrupted the oil feed to connecting-rod 2, causing its bearing to burn out together with the crankpin and thus spoil the crankshaft. This was the end of engine 7.

Test 6, with engine 9, was interrupted after half an hour wide open and 2 hours 57 minutes at 90 percent power when an exhaust valve tappet lock screw loosened on cylinder 12 and the valve dropped into the cylinder. The valve tappets then were more carefully fitted and all lock screws were wired to prevent loosening. A new start was made but the test was interrupted after 25 minutes of the second five-hour period when the A.C. Titan spark plugs began to leak badly. All plugs then were replaced by a complete set of Bethlehem Aviation plugs.

FIGURE 18.—Cylinder head casting of Curtiss K-12, 1919, with cylinder sleeves, camshafts, and valve gear assembled. (Smithsonian photo A-4602A.)

The test was discontinued after 51 minutes of the third five-hour period
when two rear camshaft bearings and three teeth of the reduction gear
on the crankshaft broke.

The report ended on an optimistic note: "The design of the engine is
excellent and it is believed to be capable of passing the 50 hrs test
without difficulty when the troubles mentioned are overcome." The
results of the different tests showed an average power of 389 hp at
2,250 rpm and a maximum of 418 hp at 2,550 rpm. Compression ratio
was 5.5:1. In the official report the engine was mentioned as Kirkham-
Curtiss model D–1200, rated at 375 bhp at 2,250 rpm.

Toward the end of 1918, or very early in 1919, two new engines,
numbers 14 and 15, were sent to the engineering division at McCook
Field to be submitted again to a 50-hour endurance test. Engine 14
broke its crankshaft during the preliminary calibration test, so only
engine 15 was given a test, which is described in McCook's Serial Report
811 of 25 April 1919. At the request of the Curtiss Company, the
engines were not run above 2,400 rpm, which was about the peak of
the power curve. The average rated power was 396 bhp at 2,250 rpm,
with a maximum of 406 hp at 2,420 rpm.

The report concluded with the statement that the engine, even though
well designed and of high power for its weight, appeared to be somewhat complicated and of difficult maintenance. The tested engine
suffered from water leaks throughout the duration of the tests, which
terminated with a cracked cylinder jacket. The report ended on a note

25

FIGURE 19.—Curtiss Eagle, 1919, powered by three Curtiss K-6 engines. (Smithsonian photo A-4602E.)

less optimistic than the previous one: "The [K–12] engine is still in the experimental stage and is not as yet suitable for actual service."

It has sometimes been stated that the K–12 was turned down because the government was concentrating on the Liberty engine. This is only partly true. The United States Navy retained its interest throughout the K–12 engine's career. Besides, the Curtiss Company never had been associated with the design or production of the Liberty. Undoubtedly it would have, had it not believed that it had something better. A great part of the millions of dollars spent on the American aeronautical effort was poured into the simultaneous attempts to mass-produce and improve the Liberty engine, a high-power design based on proved constructions. Though these efforts made it possible for America to get aero engines to the battlefront before November 1918, when the Armistice occurred, the men actively connecetd with the K–12 never could shake off the belief that the United States would have had a superior product had a fraction of the millions been put into the development of Kirkham's aluminum-block design.

After the Armistice, the interest in experimental airplanes and engines waned rapidly, and no new contracts were made for development or

26

FIGURE 20.—Curtiss Oriole for Amundsen polar expedition, with Curtiss K-6 engine, 1922. (Smithsonian photo A-4602F.)

production of the K–12; however, existing contracts were not canceled.

With the advent of peace, men were confident that weapons would be abolished for all time and the aviation manufacturers were eager to get going with plans for new commercial aircraft, of which great things were expected. The Curtiss Company, for one, brought out a beautiful new trimotor transport, the Eagle, that was powered by three 150-hp K–6 engines (Figure 19). Another use for the lower-stressed, direct-drive K–6 was found in a new three-seat sports plane, the Oriole (Figure 20), Which was also available with the war-surplus OX–5.

Curtiss President Willys was even more anxious now to get the K–12 past its teething troubles and to turn it into a salable product. He decided to call Finlay Robertson Porter to assist Kirkham in bringing the costly experiments with the K–12 to an end as soon as possible. In 1918 Porter had been chief motor engineer at McCook Field, and he had acquired some reputation in the automobile field. Porter and Wright's chief engineer, Crane, were old competitors. They had marketed, respectively, the FRP and the Crane-Simplex, the two most expensive motor cars built in the United States during 1916. Porter also was an old acquaintance of Willys, having worked with him in 1915 on a racing car powered by a Knight engine.

But Kirkham was not willing to accept any kind of assistance or supervision. The antagonism thus created between him and the Curtiss management culminated in his resignation from the Curtiss Corporation early in 1919. He then founded his own firm, Kirkham Products, which was devoted to consulting engineering in aeronautics and which would be responsible for a number of highly original airplanes and engines. His assistant chief engineer, T. S. Kemble, left Curtiss in April. Kirkham was retained for a time as consultant at Curtiss's Garden City plant to advise on the triplane, the trials of which were continuing; but his connection with the K–12 was severed forever, and Curtiss no longer was to use his name in relation to the design or use of the engine. The fate of the K–12 came completely under the responsibility of Porter, who became chief motor engineer at Curtiss.

About twenty K–12 engines had been built and several of these were still around; so, when the first big postwar aero show opened in Madison Square Garden on 1 March 1919 the K–12, rated at 375 hp, was exhibited on the Curtis stand. The Army's 18–B, now with the name Hornet, also was shown. For the Hornet, a maximum speed of 163 mph was claimed, and a speed of 80 mph was mentioned for normal use, which needed much less than half the maximum engine power. It perhaps was piously hoped that the K–12, if sold, would not be used too much at full throttle. At that time there were no type certifications or FAA inspections, and manufacturers were free to offer any product; but there is no record of any person or any service in the United States buying one of those "fastest planes in the world," as they then undoubtedly were, nor was the K–12 sold for installation in any other civil or military airplane in the United States during that year.

Through vigorous publicity and the efforts of a special sales delegation some commercial success was achieved in South America. One K–12 was installed in a triplane flying boat, ex-Navy A-2277, which was used for exploration, and one K–12-powered 18–T triplane was sold to the Bolivian government, of which more later.

The 18–T triplane had been given the name Wasp, and, by one of fate's tricks, the names Wasp and Hornet were the very ones that would be assigned to the two engines that were to cause, eight years later, the displacement of the K–12's successors in military airplanes.

It had been an idea of Chief Test Pilot Roland Rohlfs, who remained enthusiastic about the triplane's climbing abilities, that an attempt could easily be made to win the world's altitude record. Triplane A-3325 (or possibly A-3326), still in abeyance at the Curtiss Garden City plant, was converted for that purpose with enlarged two-bay

FIGURE 21.—Curtiss 18-T Wasp with Curtiss K-12 engine, destined for Bolivian air force, October 1919. (Smithsonian photo A-4602G.)

wings. A specially prepared K–12 with a higher compression ratio was used. When the first attempts were made, two or three engines burned out because the scavenging oil pump in the forward part of the engine failed to work at a high angle of climb.

In July 1919 an altitude of 30,500 ft was reached, and finally, on 18 September, with engine 13— –which had produced 465 bhp at 2,600 rpm on a compression ratio of 6:1 during a bench test in January—Rohlfs attained a height of 34,910 ft and claimed a world's record. The first part of the climb was made with a nursed engine until 31,000 ft was reached, but then, due to the steep climbing angle maintained and the lessened density of the air, the plane began to stall and dropped 600 ft. Rohlfs then applied full throttle and lowered the angle of climb for the remaining 4,000 ft. This record was never officially recognized as a world's record by the Fédération Aéronautique Internationale, apparently because the barograph, after the necessary corrections, did not show a sufficient improvement over the preceding record, made on a French Nieuport with a special high-compression Hispano-Suiza of 300 hp.

29

The climbing and high-flying demonstrations of the Wasp triplane were decisive in convincing the Bolivian authorities of the worth of that aircraft. They were anxious to have an air force like everybody else, but had been confronted by the problem of having their capital city high in the Andes mountains, with its airfield, El Alto, situated at 13,500 ft above sea level. Prior to the Bolivian government's purchase of the Curtiss Wasp (Figure 21), and in spite of some earnest attempts, no airplane had been able to take off from that airfield, but with the arrival of the K–12-powered triplane the situation changed dramatically. On 17 April 1920, in the able hands of Donald Hudson, who was on loan from the Curtiss Company to the Bolivian government, the Wasp took off from El Alto with such ease and grace that the assembled officials were wildly enthusiastic. The Bolivian Air Force was created on the spot, and Donald Hudson was made a lieutenant colonel and chief pilot.

The first flights in Bolivia were phenomenal. A short time after the first take-off Hudson reached 31,000 ft, and on 12 June he crossed the Andes, flying at 30,000 ft. Unfortunately, the elation was not to last long. In the following year, on 19 May 1921, Hudson made an over-land flight of 160 miles to Oruro in 75 minutes, but on the return flight the inevitable happened—the K–12 gave up, and the plane crashed and was destroyed beyond repair, but with no injury to the pilot. The Bolivians, who by now had become aware of the experimental status of their purchase, did not accept the loss graciously; they felt cheated, and the contract with Hudson and Curtiss was canceled. Five years later, however, relations with Curtiss became cordial again when Jimmy Doolittle flew a Curtiss Hawk fighter to El Alto field and sold several such craft to the Bolivian government.

Development of the Curtiss C-12

Meanwhile, the Curtiss Company, under the presidency of John North Willys, was not sure how to proceed with the K–12. Apart from the preparations for the height-record attempts, it appeared unlikely that more work would be devoted to that engine.

In the summer of 1919 Clement Keys, Curtiss's vice president, began a tour of Europe as a member of the American aviation mission. On that trip he visited the most important aircraft and engine manu-

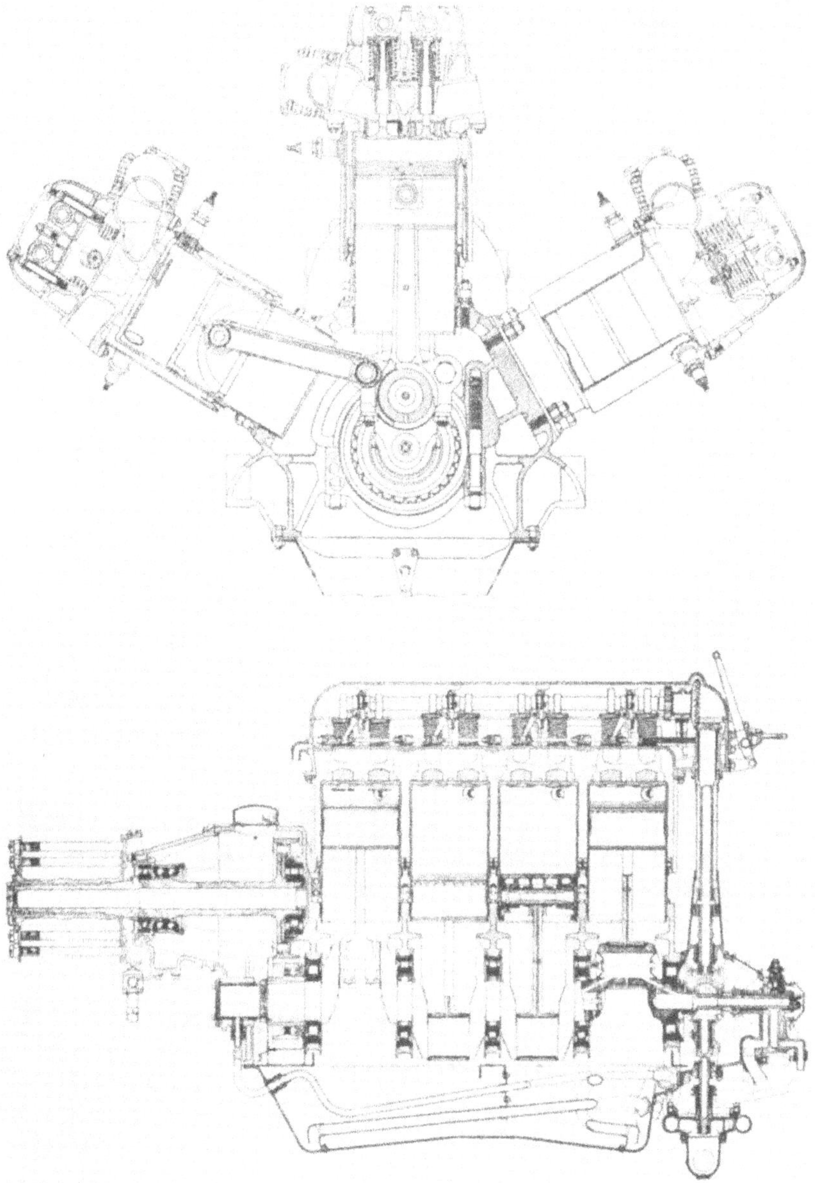

FIGURE 22.—Sectional drawings of Napier Lion, 450 hp, 1919.
(Smithsonian photo A-4619.)

31

facturers in England and France, and he quickly became aware of some interesting situations in regard to aero engine development. In England, for instance, development of water-cooled engines had virtually stopped, except for the broad-arrow Napier Lion (Figure 22), and any money made available was being spent on perfecting the high-power air-cooled radials that had been designed in 1917 and 1918. In France there was such a large stock of aero engines on hand that development had stopped altogether, and the only activity was concentrated on maintaining normal standards of reliability for the number of such engines as were needed. The leading engine there was the 300-hp Hispano-Suiza, the same model that was being readied for service by Wright Aeronautical in the United States.

Keys discovered that no engine in Europe could match the K–12 in regard to power, low weight, and small size. Also, he saw that several French airplane manufacturers were adapting the new 300-hp Hispanos to modified prototype fighters for attacks on the world's speed record, set in 1913. Indeed, that record was broken in October 1919 by a Nieuport-powered, specially prepared single-seater with clipped wings that flew at 167 mph. In contrast, the 162 mph attained by the Curtiss triplane in full military trim showed the promise of the K–12 for speed work, even if it was not then adaptable for commercial use. Keys argued that the speed record should be brought to America, and he wrote to Willys that he thought it advisable to continue the development of the K–12, the fate of which was hanging in the balance.

In April 1919 Porter had started on his assignment at the Garden City plant; and in May he took over direction of the operations in Buffalo, where the K–12 was being tested under direction of Arthur Nutt, the firm's young motor test engineer of whom we will hear more. Porter took a good look at the K–12, was able to form an opinion about the principal weaknesses of the design, and proceeded to redesign the engine accordingly.

The changes introduced in Porter's new design thus were a reflection of the experiences with the K–12. The large aluminum casting was eliminated by separating the cylinder block from the crankcase and bolting them together, which was more in accordance with Hispano practice. This arrangement eliminated the tooling problems that had appeared with the integral castings, and it eased maintenance to some extent because repairs to any cylinder could now be handled by removing a cylinder block instead of removing the whole engine, which the K–12 type of casting demanded.

The crankshaft was changed to a seven-bearing type and the counterweights of the K–12 crankshaft were eliminated, but since the cylinder

FIGURE 23.—Views of Curtiss C-12, 400 hp, 1920.
(Smithsonian photos A-4881C, A-4879.)

33

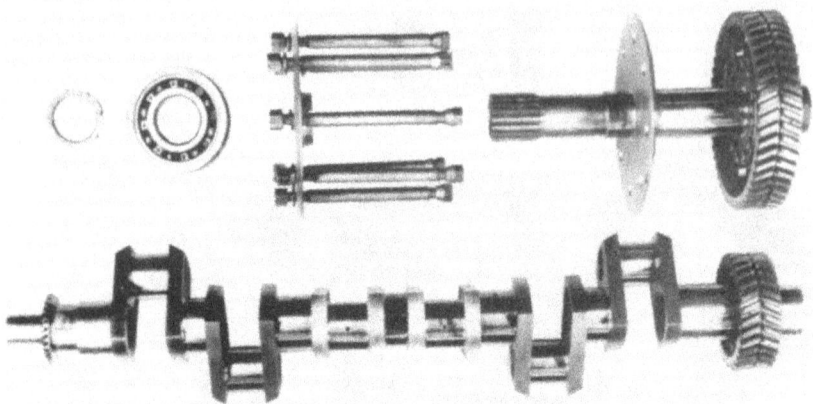

FIGURE 24.—Crankshaft, reduction gear, propeller shaft, and propeller hub of Curtiss C-12, 1921. (Smithsonian photo A-4619F.)

blocks were not redesigned the total bearing surface could not be augmented. Consequently, the introducing of more bearings was largely a step backwards.

The spark plugs, which on the K–12 had been placed side by side on the inside of the V, were relocated to both sides of the cylinder block so that six plugs were on the outside and six on the inside of each cylinder bank facing each other. Now, the failure of a magneto would not cause the loss of half engine power as with the K–12.

New carburetors of the Claudel-Hobson double-inverted type were installed. The magnetos were Berkshire D–6s, each firing one A.C. plug per cylinder.

The large exhaust collector was eliminated, obviously because it burned out too easily. All the new engines and the remaining K–12 units were fitted with short individual exhaust stacks, one for each exhaust orifice, so that there were twelve stacks on each side of the engine, a distinctive feature of all Curtiss water-cooled engines ever since. One source of trouble, the reduction gearing, was retained on the new design, but there was no way to eliminate it without suffering a great reduction in power.

The new engine (Figures 23–25) became known as the C–12. It was rated at 400 hp for 2,250 rpm, and the weight, at least for the first units, was given as 675 lb, about that of the K–12. The six-cylinder K–6 was redesigned along the same lines and renamed Curtiss Six, or C–6. It had a rating of 160 bhp at 1,750 rpm and was to have a long and successful life, without further modifications.

34

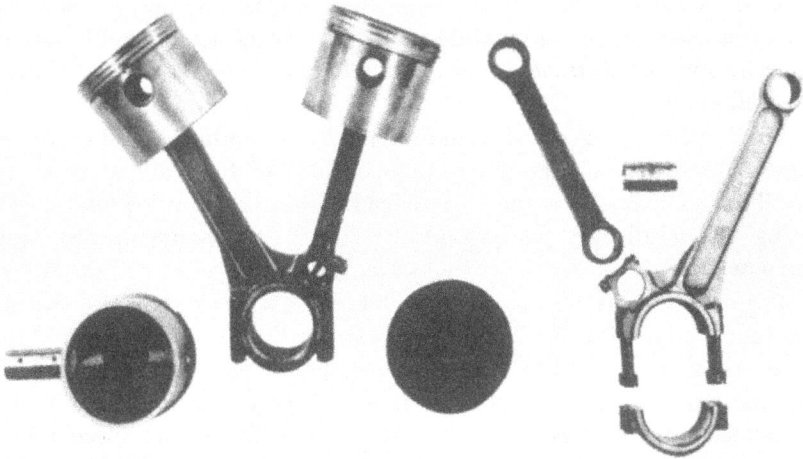

FIGURE 25.—Pistons and connecting rods of Curtiss C-12, 1921.
(Smithsonian photo A-4624G.)

The first C–12 engines were ready at the end of 1919, and the first unit was tested in January 1920. With the commercial market still in mind, Curtiss gave the new engine its first publicity showing at the New York aero show in March 1920 as the power plant of a new version of the Eagle transport, the Eagle II—the same airplane that had flown in 1919 as a trimotor with three K–6 engines. The airplane made its new appearance with two C–12 engines installed.

Roland Rohlfs piloted the new Eagle for one test flight, but during take-off the shaft driving the water pump seized on the left engine, which then lost all power within seconds. The plane barely cleared a building, actually rolling its wheels on the roof. This was the only flight of the Eagle II, as the C–12 engines were removed immediately. But it was not the end of the Eagle. In 1920, when the commercial value of the new projects was beginning to appear doubtful, the Eagle was offered to the Army for use in a project for a day-bomber with a single Liberty engine. Three such bombers were ordered, and the existing Eagle was immediately converted with a single Liberty engine and delivered to Mitchell Field. No others were built.

About the time the Eagle II made its unsuccessful test flight, both Willys and Porter were becoming convinced that there was no future in the development of high-powered aero engines, which apparently were unwanted. The Liberty had stolen a march on all new designs, and there were too many Liberties in storage. Both men withdrew

35

from the Curtiss Company to devote their talents and energies toward the promotion of the automobile industry. Porter again would market America's most expensive motor car, the Porter. The products of Willys are well known.

The C–12 was to be saved from oblivion by the enthusiasm of Clement Keys, Curtiss's new president. Keys decided to bury all attempts at possible commercial use and to go ahead with a program for high-speed flying, using all the qualities of the new C–12 engine toward that purpose.

The first important opportunity for the C–12 to show its mettle presented itself with the first postwar race for the Gordon Bennett Cup. This event, to be held in France in the summer of 1920, promised to become one of international importance. Each competing country was permitted three entries. The race itself was to be a pure speed event over a course of 300 km (186.5 miles). Each contestant could choose the time of day for his entry.

For Curtiss, the winning of the Gordon Bennett Cup was particularly desirable, as a Curtiss plane and engine had won the first such event in 1909 and derived much prestige from it. Officials at Curtiss decided to make a special effort, and the victory appeared well within reach because the decisive element, the engine, already was at hand.

A special committee met in March 1920 at a luncheon in Dayton at the invitation of Texas oil millionaire and aviation enthusiast S. E. J. Cox, who already had entered an airplane under the auspices of the Aero Club of Texas. A contract between Cox and the Curtiss Corporation that called for the building of a racer capable of at least 200 mph was signed on 19 June.

Apart from Curtiss, two other contestants from 'the United States entered racers that represented completely different approaches to the problem of obtaining high speed. An entry by the United States Army Air Service represented the expression of the "power is everything" philosophy. This was a Verville VCP pursuit biplane, originally built to carry the 300-hp Hispano but for this occasion fitted with Packard Engineering Vice-President Jesse Vincent's latest masterpiece, a 12-cylinder blockbuster based on the Liberty but displacing 2,025 cubic inches. At McCook Field the new engine had been thoroughly tuned, the compression raised, and a special fuel concocted, resulting in a power on the bench of well over 600 bhp. The reformed pursuit, designated the VCP–R, was declared capable of 200 mph.

The third American entry reflected the other extreme of design. In this airplane, built at the Dayton-Wright Company where Orville

FIGURE 26.—Curtiss-Cox Texas Wildcat, 1920, with Curtiss C-12 engine, 400 hp. (Smithsonian photo A-4619A.)

Wright was consultant, extreme fineness of penetration had been the goal, making up for a lack of engine power. The Dayton-Wright racer was a full cantilever monoplane with wings of variable camber. The engine, built by Hall-Scott, was a six-cylinder, in-line Liberty of maximum 250 hp, making this racer the lowest powered airplane entered—but the in-line engine permitted the least possible frontal area. Another special feature was the retractable undercarriage, a novelty at this time. The pilot was enclosed so completely in the fuselage that he had limited visibility, only through a window at each side. This racer, like the VCP–R, was advertised as being capable of 200 mph.

Curtiss, of course, had the C–12, giving 427 hp at 2,250 rpm—without even being pushed very much—and capable of good durability with full-throttle running. Not content to play up only the engine, Curtiss also gave the airframe maximum attention—perhaps too much. Under the direction of William Gillmore, the Curtiss engineers, carried away by the prevailing high spirits, designed and built two extremely small racers around the C–12 engine. Mrs. Cox named them Texas Wildcat and Cactus Kitten (Figures 26, 27). The first flight was made on 25 July, five weeks after the signing of the Cox contract. As usual, the undauntable Roland Rohlfs was in the cockpit. With large test wings, a speed of 183 mph was reached, but a special minimum-surface wing already was in the works and with these special race wings the maximum speed was calculated as 214 mph. These were certainly the fastest airplanes of their time, and the Gordon Bennett Cup appeared as good as won. As events turned out, one of the Curtiss racers easily could have won with the large test wings or any sort of wings, but such was the furore aroused

37

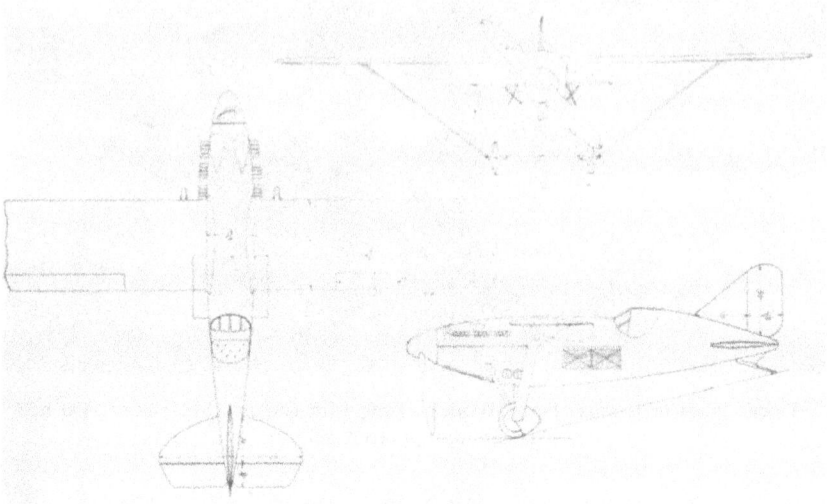

FIGURE 27.—Drawings of general arrangement of Curtiss-Cox Cactus Kitten, 1920, powered by Curtiss C-12 engine. (Smithsonian photo A-21253.)

by the press that it was thought to be of no use to enter a racer not capable of at least 200 mph.

The first tests of the Curtiss racers were held at Roosevelt Field, which was not large enough to test the maximum-speed wings. As time was runing out, the decision was made to ship the two planes to France, in the belief that the big, smooth airfields near Paris would make testing and adjusting easy. After the usual delays with shipping and customs, the machines arrived at their assigned airfield, still in crates, a bare ten days before the race. After another five days of work the Texas Wildcat was ready for a first test and Roland Rohlfs took his place at the controls.

The C–12 was started and warmed up. Soon Rohlfs gave the signal and applied full throttle, but at once he found himself in a distressing situation. The geared-down, fixed-pitch propeller had been calculated to pull hard at 200 mph, but at zero airspeed its pull was hardly noticeable. Add to this the effect of wings which did not lift until an impressive speed was reached, and the result can readily be imagined. The engine roared its utmost but the start was frustratingly slow.

Rohlfs used up the entire length of the airfield and an adjoining piece of farmland before he finally was able to get the unwilling plane airborne. He continued at a slight climb until the airplane reached a high speed and became fairly controllable. Under continuining full

38

throttle the Wildcat accelerated still more until suddenly, above 190 mph, it went into an oscillating up-and-down motion of such violence that Rohlfs had to land as soon as he could. Again the plane overshot the field, and to all intents and purposes the Curtiss racers appeared to be out of the race.

The C–12 never had missed a beat during the long take-off and the high-speed run, and it had demonstrated that it was fully dependable. So the race manager, Mike Thurston, one of the design engineers who had accompanied the planes, decided to have another try. In his hotel room that night he laid out plans for a completely new set of biplane wings and empennage, and arranged with the men of the Morane-Saulnier plant, whose airfield was being used, to manufacture them. The Texas Wildcat had the new wings and tail surfaces on the afternoon of the day before the race. With so little time remaining it was necessary to take off and fly the aircraft to Etampes Field, 30 miles away, where the Gordon Bennet Cup race was to be held.

The Curtiss racers, however, were deficient in one other detail—the undercarriage was not fitted with shock-absorbers, and an untested new kind of Dunlop wheel, with radial spokes, was used. At near take-off speed a sudden obstruction in the field caused the Wildcat to bounce into the air, where, luckily for Rohlfs, it stayed, as the new wings were lifting beautifully. But both wheels had been so severely damaged that they collapsed when the plane touched down on Etampes Field. The airplane turned over and broke in two near the cockpit. Rohlfs, of whom it truly might be said that he feared God but not the products of the Curtiss Company, was saved miraculously by his parachute pack and by the fact that a minimum supply of petrol had been carried for the short flight. The other Curtiss racer had been left in its crate. So ended the high hopes of the Curtiss people to win the Gordon Bennett Cup in 1920. Through no fault of its own, the C–12 had lost an opportunity to show again what small size and high power were worth for speed.

The two other American entries showed up no better; they reached the starting line, but the Verville had to land soon after take-off because the big Packard overheated so badly that the pilot, Rudolph ("Shorty") Schroeder, expected to see his plane go up in flames. The hurried landing proved to be a blessing, as the fuselage later was found to be cracked so severely that the tail certainly would have come off at the first turn. The other American entry, Dayton-Wright, was found to be unable to turn to the left and had to withdraw, never to be raced again.

So ends the story of a formidable American effort that gave the

Frenchmen the fright of their lives. The race itself turned out to be a surprising anticlimax. Of twelve aircraft entered, only six were present on race day. The remaining two Americans were out at once, and the result was a lone French win at 168.5 mph. A second French racer also reached the finish, but only after two forced landings and in sorry condition. Its average speed was 112 mph. A Liberty-engined DH–4 would have done better! The postrace reports pointed out how extraordinarily delicate were these high-power engines as soon as anything like a sustained effort was demanded of them. The engines in the three French racers and in the lone British contender all were 300-hp Hispano-Suizas.

In the course of the year 1920, in a competition between the French SPAD and Nieuport companies with racers that were all equipped with the 300-hp Hispano, the absolute speed record was pushed upward from 171.5 to 194.5 mph, at which mark the record stood on 31 December.

The Pulitzer race, the next high-speed event after the Gordon Bennett fiasco, was won by the same Verville VCP–R racer with the Packard engine that had proved so unmanageable in France, but this time the engine was throttled down to 1,700 rpm and the average speed achieved was 158.5 mph. A 300-hp Wright-Hispano-powered MB–3 Army pursuit plane was second, only 8 mph slower than the winner. The two K–12-powered triplanes proved very fast but both dropped out with engine trouble—one because of the breaking of a so-called main engine part, possibly the crankshaft, though no exact information has been obtained. This then was the end of the K–12 as far as service flying was concerned. A year later the K–12 made one surprisingly effective racing appearance, of which more mention will be made.

Regarding the C–12, during 1920 there was an increasing awareness of the qualities peculiar to that type of engine—a high rate of rotation and low weight coupled to a very small frontal area—and of the possible uses of those qualities for attaining very high flying speeds.

The whole theory was admirably expounded by Grover Loening in an article which vividly describes the benefits to be gained from engines with low frontal area.[1] Loening was an early champion of small fuselages, and he knew what he was taking about. In 1919 he had demonstrated that at 160 mph a 400-hp Liberty had less effective power than a 300-hp Hispano because the Liberty's greater frontal area used up 128 hp more to propel a plane at that speed than did the Hispano.

---

[1] Grover Cleveland Loening, "Engine Shape as Affecting Airplane Operation." S.A.E. Journal, vol. 6, no. 6 (20 June, 1920), pp. 417-421.

In his article, Loening referred to the then-current sentiment in aviation circles that small and fast airplanes should be powered by light, powerful, radial engines cooled by air, while water-cooled engines, mainly regarded as heavy and bulky but reliable power plants, were best suited for slow carriers of high payloads This, wrote Loening, was an error; and he referred to the formula $R=KSV2$ which gives the relation of power to speed, where K is a constant, dependent upon the shape of the airplane and for all contemporary fuselages of about the same value, and where S represents the cross-sectional or frontal area.

Loening explained that the importance of factor S should be plain to everybody, but he applied himself to convince the doubters by a clear example based on some reasoning of his own. As a standard he chose a theoretical airplane powered by the C–12 engine (which shows plainly enough whose inspiration had enligtened him), said airplane having a theoretical maximum speed of 232 mph. If, he went on, the weight of the engine, by some laborious work, were reduced to half the original amount (a fact of nearly impossible achievement, he hastened to add) the maximum speed of that airplane would be raised from 232 to 241 mph. If, on the other hand, the head resistance of the engine were halved, and the weight remained the same, the maximum speed would take a jump to 290 mph. This showed how much more important the head resistance is than the weight, and he urged builders to abandon the unwarranted race for lighter weight per horsepower and suggested that they start afresh on a new line offering far greater possibilities by making the shape of the engines more suitable to smaller airplanes.

A statistical table in Loening's article included data for the frontal areas of several contemporary engines, giving the value for the 650-hp Rolls-Royce Condor as 7.32 square feet, for the air-cooled 400-hp Bristol Jupiter radial as 12.65, the 450-hp Napier Lion as 5.68, the 400-hp Liberty as 5.16, the 420 hp Curtiss C–12 as 4.66, and the 300-hp Hispano-Suiza as 4.75. The C–12 clearly was well ahead where horsepower per square foot of frontal area was concerned. This tabulation is interesting because sooner or later all the engines mentioned would be in competition with the successors of the C–12. It was, of course, equally important to include the frontal area of the radiators, and this also had been anticipated by Kirkham when the 18–B and 18–T fighters—and later the Cox racers—had their radiators installed on the sides of the fuselages.

The C–12 could not be blamed for the unlucky outcome of the Gordon Bennett attempt in 1920, even though it still was not fit for service use. The armed forces again were becoming increasingly inter-

41

ested in what was still potentially a formidable engine for a pursuit plane. Toward the end of 1920, C–12 engine 4, probably the last built, was sent to McCook Field for evaluation and testing. McCook Field was the seat of the engineering division of the United States Army Air Force and a rather impressive concentration of engineering talent had been gathered there under Captain (later Major) George Hallett. The general idea prevailed that the engineering division should design the armed forces' own aircraft and engines, using the industry solely for production with contracts to the lowest bidder, an idea which may have resulted more from lack of funds than from self-confidence.

At McCook the C–12 was received with curiosity, and with quite a show of interest, too, as several engineers, notably William Warner and Glenn Angle, were former Curtiss engineers who had worked under Kirkham on the layout of the K–12 engine before they came to McCook Field in 1918. Captain Hallett had been chosen to accompany Lieutenant Cyril Porte as technical expert on the Wanamaker-Curtiss transatlantic flight of 1914, which had been canceled because of the outbreak of the war. In fact, everybody concerned had heard since 1918 of the "super" engine that was being developed at Buffalo.

The tests of the C–12 at McCook Field formed the basis of Serial Report 1780 of 25 November 1921. The engine had been submitted to preliminary tests for obtaining data on power, fuel consumption, and general efficiency. No run exceeded one hour, and there was no attempt to have the engine undergo a test of some duration because, when stripped after the calibration test, it was found to have suffered more than normal wear—especially in the reduction gearing—with the propeller gear teeth showing uneven wear. The reduction gearing still was the weak part of the engine, as no unit had been able to withstand more than 25 hours running.

Another weakness concerned oil consumption, which was much too high and had caused fouling of the A.C. spark plugs on the outside of the cylinder banks. These plugs were replaced with Mosler mica plugs which gave satisfaction at first but overheated quickly and caused preignition; so, they, in turn, were replaced with A.C. plugs. A slight water leakage also was observed. The cause of the excess oil consumption was traced, in part, to the seven 1-in. bearings which were too narrow for long life and proper control of the oil flow.

The inverted Claudel-Hobson carburetors were severely criticized. They gave low fuel consumption, but only at full-power operation. At lower engine speeds the specific consumption rose very quickly and there was danger of flooding and fire because of the external air vents.

The report ended with the statement that the Army's engineering division was not interested in a geared engine of this size that could not be adapted to cannon mounting. Tests of such a cannon engine had been going on since 1919 with an H-type Wright-Hispano, but never with successful results.

The C–12 tested, rated at 400 hp/2,250 rpm, was shown to give a maximum of 427 bhp at 2,250 rpm on a compression ratio of 5.5:1. The weight of the tested engine was 698 lb, or 712 lb with the necessary auxiliaries. No attempt was made to run the engine at speeds over 2,300 rpm.

Development of the Curtiss CD-12

It was by the Curtiss Company rather than by the military that the policy in regard to the future development of the C–12 was to be shaped. After Porter left, the company for a while was again without an engineer in charge of motor development, but then an engineer of supreme ability took over—Arthur Nutt, who would influence decisively the C–12's future career.

Arthur Nutt had entered the Curtiss Company after his graduation in 1918, and in July of that year he started in the experimental motor department as test observer; and later, as test engineer, he became intimately connected with the development of the K–12. In 1919, after Kirkham left, he became motor engineer under Porter and finally, after Porter's resignation, he was appointed chief motor engineer in charge of engine development. His talents were linked with Curtiss engines until the 1929 merger and then with Wright engines until October 1944 when, as Dr. Nutt, he resigned from his position as vice-president of Wright Aeronautical to join the Packard Motor Car Company. He remained with Packard until it discontinued its aircraft engine activities in 1949.

When Arthur Nutt assumed charge of the engine department at Curtiss he was only 26 years old. Yet, since the future of the company's only high-power product, the C–12, was at stake, he was at once called upon to make some important decisions and to offer advice on other questions.

Clearly, the needs of Curtiss were to stop costly experimenting and to start selling, or else abandon the C–12 design entirely. The first step, which was to be reached in the shortest possible time, was to make the

FIGURE 28.—Arthur Nutt (1895–).

C–12 reliable enough to stand an official 50-hour test and then sell it to the only available customers, the armed services. It was obvious that with the enormous amount of cheap Liberty engines around there was no question of entering a nearly nonexistent commercial market. Even the Eagle had ended by being powered with a Liberty engine.

Arthur Nutt put forth his ideas after consultation with William Gillmore, chief aeronautical engineer. The Curtiss management agreed that there was no time to develop the reduction gearing to suitable reliability, so the best and only thing to do was to dispense with the gears altogether. This entailed a lowering in rotational speed of the crankshaft to retain propeller efficiency and, in fact, a complete derating, which would further increase reliability.

The Curtiss officials were confident that even in derated form the C–12 would still remain a competitive product. Without reduction gears it would weigh 650 lb, against the 300-hp Wright-Hispano's 625 lb and Liberty's 850 lb, which, in high-compression form, gave a very theoretical maximum of 420 bhp. The decision to derate the C–12 could, of course, have been taken much earlier, and even applied to the K–12, but the continuous obsession with highest power had prevented it heretofore.

Both services were interested in the design but were then severely

44

short of funds, so an agreement was reached to divide the expense of the development of the new model. The Navy agreed to buy one derated C–12, whose power was provisionally taken from a point down the original K–12 curve and set at 325 hp at 1,800 rpm crankshaft speed. The Army agreed to do the testing at McCook Field, and to participate in the development; thus, it would both gain experience and help pay its share of the costs.

On 19 October 1920 a supplemental agreement was signed with Curtiss by the Navy, amending contract 46553 for one C–12 engine without reduction gears at a total cost of $31,000—no small sum for an aero engine at that time. Contract 46553 had been pending with Curtiss since 1918 for the furnishing of four K–12 engines, but because none of those engines had passed its official acceptance test a report of September 1920 still mentioned that contract as zero percent completed. The rating of 325 hp was quite acceptable to the Navy, whose low-compression Liberty engines had an output of about 330 hp at sea level and were much bigger and heavier than the C–12.

The first C–12 Direct-Drive, or CD–12, as the engine was renamed, was shipped from the Curtiss plant to McCook Field for testing on 25 February 1921. It differed from a C–12 only by having all of its spark plugs on the inside of the V, doubtless to avoid the oil fouling of the plugs on the outside of the cylinder banks, from which the C–12 had suffered. The rest of the design was kept unchanged, even as to the Claudel carburetors. (Figure 29.)

There was some bickering at first between the Army and the Navy over the duration of the test to which the new engine should be submitted. The Navy insisted on 60 hours but the Army contended that 50 hours was enough. A telegram dated 9 March states that if there was no agreement on 50 hours the Army would ship the engine immediately to the Navy and proceed with work on the geared C–12, from which it appears that the engineering division at McCook Field was still hoping to see the C–12 brought to satisfactory status. It was finally agreed that the engine would be submitted to a preliminary ten-hour test for the Navy, followed by a normal 50-hour test for the Army. These tests are described in McCook Serial Report 1853, dated 10 January 1922.

The ten-hour run for the Navy was made on a low-compression ratio of 5.23:1 in two of the usual five-hour periods. The test of CD–12 engine 1 (Bureau Number 9673) started on 4 April and was completed on 21 April 1921. The power developed on the dynamometer prior to the start of the ten-hour test was 335 bhp at the normal speed of 1,800 rpm, 360 bhp at 2,000 rpm, and 368 bhp at 2,100 rpm. After 8 hours

57 minutes running, the failure of a spring collar retaining nut caused one of the intake valves to drop into number 3 cylinder. The repair was made and three new cam followers were installed at the same time. The ten-hour test for the Navy then ran to completion.

After this test the engine was torn down for complete inspection prior to the 50-hour Army endurance test, and it was found to be still in excellent condition. This gave rise to an optimistic mood, and it was decided to let the 50-hour endurance test be run under more severe conditions. The compression would be raised by installing different pistons and the normal speed would be 2,000 rpm instead of 1,800. The Army 50-hour test started on 4 May and ended 24 June. It was the first 50-hour test to be completed since the inception of the design four years earlier.

At the end of each five-hour period the engine was stopped and checked and minor adjustments were made when necessary. Because of the higher power developed and the duration of the test, the engine did not do as well as in the Navy test. During the warmup two of the new high-compression pistons seized. It was found that the compression ratio was 5.65:1, and, as this appeared too high, all the pistons were again replaced with ones giving a compression of 5.37:1.

In the course of the test there were numerous forced stops, and advantage was taken during these times to redesign or strengthen all the parts that failed, though all major parts held. The performance of the engine remained good and it ran very smoothly throughout the test.

During the calibration test, preliminary to the endurance test, the power developed at the normal speed of 2,000 rpm was 383 bhp; the maximum reached was 393 bhp at 2,090 rpm. The average power developed during the full-throttle runs of the 50-hour test was 367 bhp at 1,976 rpm. The fuel and oil consumption was good. When the engine was torn down for final inspection after the tests it was discovered that two of the lower bearing caps had failed just before the end of the test, but the bearings were still in very good condition. The overall wear of the engine, especially of the valves, was such that the engine would have been due, shortly afterwards, for a complete overhaul.

The Navy had at once placed an order for two more CD–12 engines (Contract 53933) destined for new service aircraft in replacement of the Wright-H (the 300-hp Wright-Hispano), but plans soon were formed to use the CD–12 for racing. This shows that even then, in derated form, the CD–12 was thought to be an unbeatable proposition for high-speed work. The ordering of two new racing aircraft from Curtiss by the Navy in June 1921 may be considered to represent the opposite pole of the attitude that had led to the construction of the Cox racers and a direct

FIGURE 29.—Views of Curtiss CD-12 aero engine of 1922, which had an electric starter. (Smithsonian photos A-4781B, A-4781.)

47

result of the experience gained and the disappointments suffered at the 1920 Gordon Bennett race.

Due respect was now given to a low landing speed. The Navy had placed a ban on anything above 75 mph. The new racers, therefore, were biplanes with an appreciable wing area and, it may be presumed, with a strong landing gear. In fact, they relied nearly exclusively on the power and possibility for aerodynamic penetration of their CD–12 engines—following Loening's teaching—for the attainment of adequate speeds in competition. The history of the first Navy Curtiss racers or CR airplanes is not to be related here; suffice it to say that after ordering two planes in June the Navy lost interest but permitted one of the planes to be entered privately by the Curtiss Company for the 1921 Pulitzer races, which were held in November.

The CD–12 meanwhile had shown definite promise for improved reliable output and, by being pushed a little, had been able to develop 405 bhp at 2,000 rpm after the compression ratio had been raised to 6.1:1 by using a fuel with a high percentage of benzol. Whereas the power of the latest CD–12 had not risen above that of the original K–12, it now was achieved at 2,000 rpm instead of at 2,500, showing how appreciable an increase in mean effective pressure had been reached in two years.

The Pulitzer race of 1921 was won convincingly by the Navy Curtiss racer (Figure 30) piloted by Bert Acosta at 176 mph. Second place was taken by the other 1920 Gordon Bennett racer, the Cactus Kitten. This racer still was powered with the geared C–12, giving some 435 hp, but the airplane was changed beyond recognition by the application of a set of impressive-looking triplane wings. These, suitably clipped, had been taken from one of the early triplanes. With these wings it was hoped to keep the landing speed down to 70 mph. The Cactus Kitten appeared to be the faster of the two Curtiss entries. Its maximum speed was evaluated at 196 mph, but the CR won, due presumably to its superior handling qualities. The Cactus Kitten nevertheless achieved the fame of being the fastest triplane ever built.

Third place was taken by a Thomas Morse MB–6 powered by the inevitable competitor, the Wright-H, of well over 300 hp now. Since the previous January Wright had dropped the "-Hispano" addition to its name, showing how far the design had been Americanized; indeed, the Americanized version was fast becoming better than the French original! There was another Curtiss engine entered—an old 400-hp K–12 whose swan song this race would prove to be. Powering an Ansaldo Balilla, it had won the American Legion Derby a few days earlier, and

48

FIGURE 30.—Navy Curtiss Racer CR-1, powered by Curtiss CD-12 engine, 400 hp. This plane, piloted by Bert Acosta, won the Pulitzer trophy at Omaha, Nebraska, on 3 November 1921. (Smithsonian photo A-4624B.)

it now finished the Pulitzer race without trouble, securing fourth place.

Cox had tried to enter his repaired Texas Wildcat biplane too, but it was ruled out because of its high landing speed. The result of the race showed that three of the first four placed were powered by Curtiss engines, one of each model developed since 1918. The advantage of low frontal area, coupled with high power, again was proven conclusively.

Only four CD-12 engines had been built, and three of these were sold to the Navy. Engine 2 was retained by Curtiss as a prototype to prepare for series production, and plans and specifications were drawn up together with a comparative study of the CD-12 versus the Liberty and the Wright-H. The specifications offered the engine as the CD-12A in both a low- and a high-compression version, rated at 375 and 400 bhp respectively, both ratings at 2,000 rpm for a weight of 700 lb dry. The limit of 2,000 rpm, imposed by the propeller, could not be raised at that time.

Other than the United States Navy, there was no prospective purchaser, but in England, as early as March 1921, Frank Barnwell, the celebrated designer of the Bristol Fighter, suggested the adoption of a Bristol Scout`F airframe—hitherto powered by radial air-cooled engine types—as a flying testbed for one of the new Curtiss engines. His proposal was not accepted, but in view of the outstanding developments in Britain, to be described later, it provided a touch of the prophetic.

Two CD–12 units were used by the Navy as power plants for the new Curtiss Torpedodropper, or CT (A–5890), in replacement of the originally installed Wright-H engines which were prone to excessive vibration. The prototype CT was delivered to Anacostia in January 1922 and fitted with CD–12 engines 3 and 4, but before June both engines, one in damaged condition, had been shipped back to the Curtiss Company for reconditioning. Nine CT planes had been ordered, but by 1 July the eight remaining planes of that order were canceled as being "of doubtful value for Naval Purposes."

After the 50-hour test, CD–12 engine 1 was shipped back to Curtiss on 8 September 1921 and was the object of negotiations for converting it from a test engine into an operationally useful unit at minimum cost. The result was BuAero contract 55792 of 14 March 1922, ordering a variety of changes—including correction of the weaknesses encountered during the tests—to be made at a cost of $1,625. The principal changes were a new intake manifold, a Ball and Ball carburetor, a new water pump impeller and shaft, new camshaft drive shafts, and gears of new design. During conversion it was decided to install high-compression pistons so the engine could be used for racing.

During the summer of 1922 the Navy decided to use two CD–12 engines to stage a comeback of the 18–T triplanes. These, after the breakdown of the Navy's K–12 engines at the 1920 Pulitzer races, had remained in storage and were now being reconditioned again as single-float seaplanes at the Naval Aircraft Factory in preparation for their use in competition. Their maximum speed was calculated to be 131 mph. Reconditioned engine 1 was fitted to A–3325, while one of the later engines was installed on A–3326. The two triplanes then were entered for the 1922 Curtiss Marine Trophy race on 8 October 1922. One of these, piloted by Lieutenant Sanderson, was nearing victory when it ran out of fuel in the last lap. After the race A–3325 was sent to Selfridge Field, where it was wrecked shortly afterwards. The second triplane, which remained in service for another year, will be referred to later.

A–3325's undamaged engine, CD–12 engine 1 (Bureau No. 9673), was in the Navy Museum in Philadelphia until 1926, when it was shipped to the Smithsonian Institution. This was the first engine to pass a 50-hour test at 375 bhp. Certainly it is worthy of preservation, as it pointed the way for the history-shaping engine that will now be discussed.

The Curtiss D-12 Engine

In July 1921, after the CD–12 finally showed itself capable of passing a service test, it then was possible to put the engine into production with a fair possibility of sales, which in the case of the Navy had already begun. However, the experience gained had shown Arthur Nutt and the engineering staff at McCook Field, where most of the testing of the C–12 and CD–12 had been done, that the design could be reworked into a really good engine by correcting the few basic weaknesses still remaining.

After the official test of the CD–12, the engineering division at McCook Field made several recommendations that were detailed in official letters to the Curtiss Corporation. The first such letter was dated 22 August 1921, and the Curtiss Corporation replied on 6 October; a second letter from McCook Field was dated 14 October. The principal criticisms and recommendations were as follows. (a) The crankcase and oil system should be changed to conventional dry sump. (b) The crankshaft main bearings, especially bearings 2, 4, and 6, were considered too narrow. This condition could be remedied only by lengthening the bearings or by using a four-bearing crankshaft like that on the K–12. (c) The Claudel inverted carburetor was considered unsatisfactory. An approved make of upright carburetor was recommended to be fitted inside the V of the engine and, if necessary, after redesigning the intake manifold. (The Navy had already returned to the K–12 carburetor for its first CD–12.)

The engineers at McCook Field had gone to great lengths in order to prove their points, and, as a result of a detailed study comparing the C–12 and K–12 crankshaft construction, Report 1996 was issued. This report contained a complete calculation of all the crankshaft stresses and bearing loads of the K–12, C–12, and CD–12 engines and a theoretical direct-drive KD–12 engine with a four-bearing crankshaft. The conclusions showed that Porter's seven-bearing crankshaft was inferior to Kirkham's four-bearing one because the seven bearings were of insufficient surface, especially the central bearing, the one most heavily loaded.

Kirkham later improved his crankshaft by installing more counterweights, and this improvement caused McCook Field's engineers to recommend it for future development. The K–12-type crankshaft appeared amply sufficient, especially for a direct-drive engine run at not more than 2,000 rpm.

The report by McCook Field's engineering division allowed the Curtiss engineering staff two alternatives. One alternative was the simple one of adopting the K–12-type, four-bearing crankshaft on a CD–12-type engine, and this would lead to a satisfactory 375-hp engine in the shortest possible time. The other alternative, appearing to be a longer and more arduous undertaking, was to redesign the crankshaft as a seven-bearing unit with adequate bearings for which McCook's engineering division specified the minimum lengths that would be satisfactory. This second alternative would necessitate a complete redesigning of the cylinder blocks due to the respacing of the cylinder center distances.

The difficult but more rewarding policy was chosen by Arthur Nutt. On 13 October 1921 he submitted to the engineering division at McCook preliminary drawings of a new crankshaft having adequately proportioned main bearings. The seven one-inch bearings were replaced with six bearings of 1½ inches and a central bearing of 1¾ inches. Future experience would show that the width of the new bearings was sufficient to cope with the increased loads of the later, larger-bore developments.

The cylinder blocks were completely redesigned, as were the connecting rods, the cylinder attachments, and all other accessories that had given trouble or that could be lightened without impairing reliability. The lubrication oil was taken from a separate oil reservoir through an oil cooler instead of from the crankcase sump. This construction, currently called dry-sump lubrication, would permit a smaller and stiffer crankcase, a more effective lubrication by control of the oil temperature, and a small gain in reduced frontal area.

The new design required new patterns and castings, and the new crankshaft, which was drop-forged, required the sinking of massive dies by the Wyman-Gordon Company of Worcester, Massachusetts. Carburetion also was completely modified. Frank Mock, of Stromberg, went to Buffalo in January 1922 to lay out and design a new Stromberg carburetor for the new Curtiss engine. The patterns were made at Curtiss under his supervision, while the castings, machining, and assembly were effected at the Stromberg plant. The result was the Stromberg NA–Y5, which was to become standard for all D–12 engines.

The Stromberg carburetors were not ready to be installed on the first engines in time for their tests. These engines were fitted with American Zenith 54-mm carburetors which, following the rejection of the earlier Claudels by McCook Field's engineering division, had been chosen for installation on the CD–12A engine that was not put into production. The magnetos of all early D–12 engines were Splitdorf SS–12s.

This, then, was the engine that was to achieve fame as the Curtiss D–12 and was to have a profound influence on subsequent aero engine design. At first it was regarded as an improved version of the CD–12 and was rated accordingly, 375 hp at 2,000 rpm, but it soon would show itself capable of much better outputs and much higher crankshaft speeds. The limits imposed on the propeller by the tip speed prevented higher speeds for a time, but a new development in propeller design by S. A. Reed would finally put the D–12 in a class far above its contempories.

The D–12 was not only a mechanical masterpiece; it also was a beautiful engine, with a grace that derived from the simple and yet purposeful form, and its lines set a fashion for all high-power, liquid-cooled power plants down through World War II. Henceforth, it would be impossible for any engine with individual liquid-cooled cylinders—no matter how much it might be based on up-to-date concepts—to overcome the impression of being somehow "antique."

The Navy ordered twelve engines straightaway (Bureau Contract 55824), even before the first D–12 had passed the regulation 50-hour endurance test. Two D–12s of that contract were to be delivered to the Army. This first order was followed by another in April and a third soon afterwards. By the first of July 1922 there were 57 additional engines on order under Contract 56230.

The first D–12 engines received by the Navy were rated at 350 hp at 1,800 rpm. The contract weight, limited to 720 lb with reference to the latest improved CD–12, was found to have been reduced by 52 lb. The Navy did not regard its first D–12 engines in their true capacity as power plants for high-speed or fighter airplanes but used them as a sort of smaller and improved Liberty on a series of newly evolved Torpedo or Observation aircraft which barely passed the 100-mph mark. These aircraft were the Douglas XNO 1, Martin MO–1, and Martin M2O–1; also, the Curtiss CT ended its career with two D–12 engines installed.

The Army did not relish being left with only two D–12 engines, and the Navy's monopolizing of the D–12 production was not well received. The Navy, of course, considered itself the principal beneficiary by right, as, from the K–12 onward, Curtiss high-power engine development had been under some form of Navy sponsorship while the Army had participated mostly by evaluation of design and by testing, not by actual purchases. Under an agreement eventually reached by the two services the Army Air Corps would receive 27 of the 57 engines ordered by the Navy under Contract 56230. Afterwards, production would be able to supply both services.

The first D–12 delivered to the Navy completed its preliminary acceptance tests and passed the official 50-hour endurance test between 12 April and 27 May 1922. It was submitted to an additional 250 hours of testing, as was Navy practice at the time, and then to several more full-load tests, bringing the total testing time to 275 hours on 19 July 1923. The engine then was set up at Buffalo for an additional 200-hour duration test at part load. After 88½ hours running, this test ended on 3 August when the rear left piston broke and the corresponding connecting rod assembly at once went through the crankcase and wrecked the engine. After dismantling, all remaining pistons showed cracks near the bosses, but the other parts were found in very good to excellent condition. A new stronger piston was designed for all remaining engines.

There was unforeseen delay in the acceptance of the remaining eleven engines of Contract 55824 because the Navy claimed to have found an excessive quantity of nonmetallic material in the forged crankshafts. Neither Curtiss nor the forger agreed with the Navy about this, but they had to replace the shafts.

As we have seen, the Army received in 1922 two of the first twelve engines ordered by the Navy. The Army was more alive to the potentialities of the D–12, and it was eager to test its capacity as a high-speed engine.

Two Fokker fighters, still crowned with the laurels of a famous name, then were on order by the U.S. Army Air Forces. These fighters, powered by Wright-H 300-hp engines, had been allocated Army Air Forces designations PW–5 and PW–6 (PW means "pursuit watercooled"). In August 1922 a contract was placed in Holland for a third Fokker to be designated PW–7 and powered by the D–12 engine. It was hoped that the Fokker/D–12 combination would become the most advanced fighter airplane of its time.

There also were some thoughts regarding modification of the PW–1 fighter, with its already obsolete Packard engine, so that it would accommodate the D–12 with a nose radiator, but nothing came of that.

Before the Army's first two D–12 engines were used as prototype fighter engines they showed their true pace as racing engines when two high-speed airplanes were ordered from Curtiss to compete as R–6s in the 1922 Pulitzer races, which were to be held in October at Detroit and where the D–12 would make its first public appearance. For these two new racers, the Curtiss engineers exercised utmost care to eliminate all unnecessary drag and went to the extreme of incorporating the radiators as part of the wing surfaces. Otherwise, the new Army R–6 racers were

FIGURE 31.—Curtiss R-6 Army racer powered by Curtiss D-12 engine, 450 hp, 1922. (Smithsonian photo A-4624E.)

still fully braced biplanes with fixed undercarriages (Figure 31) and low landing speeds.

The race ended in a sweeping victory for the Army and a decisive one for the D–12 which secured the first four places and was hailed as the speed champion of its time. The two Army R–6 racers, two of the most beautiful airplanes ever built, came in first and second, followed by the two Curtiss Navy racers. The winners' average speed was 206 mph, 30 mph more than the 1921 winner had achieved. The exact horsepower developed by the victorious D–12 engine was not divulged and contemporary press reports differ widely in that respect; but as a small-diameter

FIGURE 32.—Wright T-2 engine, 700 hp, about 1922. (Smithsonian photo A-4624F.)

wooden propeller capable of withstanding a speed of 2,200 rpm had been fitted, the D–12 was able to deliver the 440/450 bhp at that speed when fitted with high-compression pistons and running on a 50 percent benzol mixture.

This 1922 Pulitzer Trophy race was not only an interesting event because of the D–12's performance; it also was noteworthy for the competition that was offered by other engine manufacturers.

The greatest effort for the race had been made by the Wright Aeronautical Corporation, still the principal purveyor of fighter engines. That company had had two aces up its sleeve. The first was a refined high-compression model of its 300-hp, eight-cylinder model H that produced close to 400 bhp. These engines were fitted to several racers, two of which—Verville-Sperry R–3's with retractable landing gears and monoplane wings—finished fifth and seventh. Approximately 400 bhp would prove the maximum of which the model H engine was capable, and that engine's normal proneness to vibration was much aggravated when running with high-compression pistons. But the Wright engineers had developed their second ace, a big new V–12 of 1,950 cubic inches capacity. This engine—also of monoblock construction with dry liners, following the original Hispano-Suiza concept—had open-end sleeves and four valves per cylinder. Known as the T–2, it had already been

56

FIGURE 33.—Packard aero engine 1-A-2025, 630 hp, about 1920-1922. (Smithsonian photo A-2325.)

accepted by the Navy for heavy-duty service rated at 525 hp.

The Navy, always on the alert for healthy competition between manufacturers, had eagerly backed the construction of a Wright racing airplane to be powered by a high-compression version of the T–2 engine (Figure 32) that developed over 700 bhp. This racer, first known as the Navy Mystery because of the secrecy that surrounded its building, was a dubious monoplane or half-hearted biplane. It was built along the lines of a Nieuport racer, to which the French had applied the designation Sesquiplan, meaning one-and-a-half plane. The T–2 engine proved inadequate to demands for high power, and the Mystery was retired from the 1922 Pulitzer race after making only one lap at high speed.

Another firm still competing for honors was Packard. Its 2,025 cubic inch Gordon Bennett engine of 1920, now reliable and good for about

630 hp (Figure 33), was installed in several racers, the oldest of which was the Verville R–1 that had won the first Pulitzer Trophy in 1920. The Verville could place no better than sixth, while the other, and newer, Packard-powered racers finished in the last places. Thus, it was again brought home that brute force alone was not sufficient to win.

The 1922 Pulitzer race was to be the last appearance of the big Packard engine, as the company found that it needed something more refined if it wanted to continue in competition against the new Curtiss and Wright monoblock engines. The result was that Packard soon would make a great effort to come up with its own advanced design.

The apotheosis came a few days after the race when General Billy Mitchell, using the Army's Pulitzer winner, brought the world's speed record to the United States for the first time with a mean speed over four runs of 223 mph. Lieutenant Russell Maughan, the Pulitzer winner, had attained the unofficial speed of 220 mph before the race when testing the speed of the new plane.

Speed, that most glamorous of all records, had been pushed upwards very slowly after 1920: first to 205 mph in September 1921 by the introduction of the Nieuport Sesquiplan of high wing loading and landing speed, and a year later to 212 mph by the same Nieuport, powered by the same Hispano-Suiza and manned by the same pilot, Sadi-Lecointe, who had become a French national hero. Sadi's second record was made only a few days before Maughan reached the 220 mph mark.

Toward the end of 1922 the Army asked for bids on a new ambulance plane, and Curtiss immediately proposed the Eagle again. This ubiquitous transport already had been considered for the nonstop crossing of the American continent that was to be performed by a Fokker T–2,[2] and Curtiss now wanted to sell the Eagle as an ambulance plane with a D–12 engine. The Army concluded that the Eagle indeed appeared to be the most suitable design from a medical standpoint but, with a touch of regret, added that the planes would have to be fitted with Liberty engines because so many of these engines were on hand. And so it happened. The Liberty-powered Eagle was converted into an ambulance plane in 1923, but soon afterward its career ended in a crash.

After the Pulitzer races of 1922 the Army's two D–12 engines were removed from the racers and sent to Curtiss for reconditioning. One of the engines then was shipped to Holland for installation in the Fokker PW–7, which, with the Curtiss engine, showed a maximum speed of 151 mph, against 138 mph for the earlier two Fokkers with their 300-Wright

[2] See Louis S. Casey, "The First Nonstop Coast-to-Coast Flight and Historic T-2 Airplane," *Smithsonian Annals of Flight*, no. 1 (1964) .

engines. But the PW–7 was not to be put into production. The first new fighter built expressly around a D–12 engine was, naturally, a Curtiss product, and it received Army designation PW–8. The prototype was ready early in 1923, showing that the Curtiss designers had lost no time. The first PW–8 machine was based on the winning Pulitzer racers to the point of having wing radiators. In service trim and with a high-compression D–12 engine, it achieved a maximum speed of 170 mph.

Also in 1923, Boeing brought out the PW–9, which was to become a worthy competitor of the Curtiss fighter. The Thomas Morse Company, manufacturer of the standard Army Pursuit MB–3, received a D–12 on loan for installation in its new TM–22 prototype; but that plane was abandoned early because it proved to be too small and impossible to handle.

Wright tried to counter the success of the D–12-powered fighters with the introduction of an all-metal fighter built around the 700-hp T–3 engine. This fighter made its first flight during 1923 but was not able to out-perform the Curtiss-powered planes. The Wright competition for high-performance, aluminum-monoblock engines would soon come to an end, but Wright was to attack on another front, as its H–3 engine was to gain a belated victory over the D–12 in the struggle for the world speed record.

When the French learned that the Wright-H engines were able to deliver much more power than their own Hispano-Suizas, they took a drastic step. In 1922 they imported one of the American Wright-H engines, capable of 400 bhp at 2,000 rpm, and installed it in a new Nieuport (model 37) racer. When this plane proved unsuccesesful the Sesquiplan racer was fitted with the Wright engine, or one closely patterned after it. Wing radiators were installed, and the wings were clipped to the bare minimum with the handicap of a 112-mph landing speed. With this modified Sesquiplan, Sadi-Lecointe was able to raise the speed record in February 1923 to 233 mph and beat the American marks established in 1922.

The French record was to last only a few weeks. Early in 1923 McCook Field received the first D–12 engines fitted with the new Stromberg NA–Y5 carburetors. The Strombergs were found to be a big improvement over the earlier Zeniths as they functioned perfectly up to 2,500 rpm, while with the Zenith the D–12 would not function over 2,300 rpm. On 29 March 1923 Lieutenant Maughan established a new world's record of 244.9 mph with a biplane R–6 racer powered by the Pulitzer-winning D–12 with Stromberg carburetors and a new all-metal propeller. The new propeller was the result of the experimental work of Dr. Sylvanus Albertus

Reed, who was to add his fame to that of Dr. Nutt in helping to boost the D–12 to a new level of performance by permitting it to unleash its power at high speed without having to use the troublesome reduction gear again. In view of this development's importance, its story is included here.

In 1915, while engaged in research on high-frequency acoustics, Dr. Reed was employing an apparatus with a shaft revolving at 36,000 rpm. It occurred to him that it would be interesting to conduct similar experiments with high-speed propellers. He was fully cognizant of the problems that were believed to arise when any object moving through air approached the speed of sound, a belief based on the experience from tests conducted with artillery shells. It was known that at or near the speed of sound there is a critical point on the curve of the relation to air resistance, but Reed professed a truly scientific attitude of mind by not believing anything before it had been proven—all the more as he had been told that the subject of very high propeller tip speeds was a field that had not been explored.

Reed thought that the difficulties encountered when the speed of sound was reached might well be dependent upon the shape of the moving object. He then proceeded to conduct a long series of experiments, first with propellers 20 inches long which he revolved at 14,000 rpm—ascertaining, perhaps a bit rashly, that the supposed physical limit at the speed of sound did not exist and that the thrust of his propellers did not undergo any appreciable variation when exceeding that limit.

This was truly a revolutionary theory at that time, considering that as late as 1919 the British Advisory Committee for Aeronautics had issued an official report of its own experiments in which it was affirmed that thrust practically disappeared at high tip speeds, a conclusion corroborated by American tests conducted at McCook Field. Nevertheless, Reed was able to interest officials of the Curtiss Company in his research, especially William Gilmore, chief airplane engineer in charge of airframe design, who placed full facilities for further testing at Reed's disposal.

The final result of Reed's experiments was the Z–1 propeller of 1921, which had very thin tips and razor-sharp edges. In fact, Reed had anticipated what the aeronautical engineers would discover 25 years later when the speed of sound would be approached by full-size aerofoils. To be able to obtain the necessary thin section, the Reed propeller was made of aluminum in one forging. It gave excellent results, being capable of very high efficiency at hitherto unheard-of speeds of rotation. It became the perfect associate for the direct-drive D–12 engine, which seemed eager to turn at speeds higher than the 2,000 rpm to which it had been restricted by the older types of airscrew.

With all activity directed towards the winning of the Pulitzer races, the speed records, and the contract with Fokker, it was May 1923 before a D–12 engine could be spared for a duration test at McCook Field. The first engine to arrive was D–12 No. 22, A.S. 23–112, fitted with low-compression pistons. Shortly afterwards it was joined by the Pulitzer winner and holder of the speed record, an engine which was to be submitted to a high-compression (C.R. 5.7:1) test. The racing engine was wrecked during a preliminary fuel consumption run when a master connecting rod broke and ruined the crankcase.

The low-compression (C.R. 5.3:1) engine was submitted to a complete 50-hour test on the dynamometer (McCook Serial No. 2266). The test was conducted in July 1923, so the engineering division at McCook Field took over testing of the D–12 at the time the Navy finished its testing of that engine. The Army test was tougher than the earlier Navy ones because the engineering division at McCook Field aimed at once at high power and allowed the engine to be run at speeds up to 2,310 rpm, at which speed 428 bhp was developed. The engine stood up satisfactorily to the tests, but at the end of the performance it was found that a cylinder block had developed a light crack.

The same weakness also became apparent when a new Curtiss PW–8 fighter was used for an attempt at a flight that was to become memorable as the "dawn-to-dusk flight." This was an effort to cross the American continent during daytime, a feat that could be performed only by an engine and plane capable of maintaining racing power and speed for a long period of time, a much tougher undertaking than the short burst of speed necessary to establish a record or win a race.

The first PW–8 plane was prepared for Lieutenant Maughan, the winner of the 1922 Pulitzer race and the pilot who had established a world speed record in March 1923. Maughan took off for the big try on 10 July 1923. In contrast to the transcontinental flight of the Fokker T–2 a few months earlier, the PW–8 flight was organized with intermediary stops, but with the engine full out during the flying laps. This first attempt ended when Maughan was forced down 15 miles from the intended stop at St. Joseph, Missouri, because of a clogged gasoline line. He had covered 1,330 miles in nine hours.

A second attempt was made on 19 July. When over North Platte, Nebraska, Maughan noted that a layer of oil was forming on the cockpit floor. He flew on, and after the scheduled landing at Cheyenne, Wyoming, a leak in the oil cooler was repaired. But after taking off from Cheyenne the trouble appeared to get worse, and Maughan landed at Rock Springs, his cockpit covered with an inch-deep mixture of water and oil. He had already covered two-thirds of the total distance at racing speed. A close inspection showed that two cylinder blocks had cracked at the rear so that the engine was losing a gallon of water per minute and was on the verge of seizing. Maughan then had to postpone his gallant effort for a year.

Meanwhile, there was another challenge overseas—the race for the 1923 Schneider Trophy, a tough, high-speed event for seaplanes preceded by navigability trials. The United States Navy originally entered three planes. Two were float-mounted CR planes of 1921 and 1922 Pulitzer vintage. Each of these two aircraft was fitted with a finely tuned, high-compression D–12, a Reed propeller, and wing radiators (see Figure 34). With these modifications, the planes were designated CR–3s. The third Navy entry was the NW–1, the 1922 Mystery which had been turned into a biplane, on floats, with a Wright T–2 engine of some 700 hp.

The announcement of these entries created a stir among the traditional European participants, especially in England where a special effort had resulted in the winning of the event in 1922. For the 1923 race England entered a light Supermarine flying boat based on the 1922 winner and powered by the Napier Lion. France was relying on the 300-hp Hispano-Suiza.

The Navy's NW–1 crashed during the preliminary tests when the engine disintegrated after 20 minutes of flight. The demise of this racer left the two diminutive CR–3 seaplanes as the only American challengers. The CR–3s looked frail against the assembled flying boats of Europe, but the D–12 engine, running on a 50 percent benzol mixture, was able to turn out 475 bhp at 2,300 rpm, with the Reed propeller operating at high efficiency. The British favorite, however, with 560 bhp and a geared-down propeller, surely was not lacking in power.

The result of the race was surprising. The two D–12 engines ran perfectly and the Curtiss planes made a clean sweep, attaining speeds that left everyone stunned. The average speed of the CR–3s was 30 mph more than that of the 1922 winner and 20 mph above that of the third-placed Supermarine, which was clearly outclassed in spite of its greater power. The victory had been achieved largely through the D–12's small frontal area, high power, and uncommon reliability. This race had a profound effect on British military aircraft and engine design, as we shall see later.

The year 1923 witnessed another D–12 victory for the Navy when two Curtiss biplane racers model R2 C–1, powered by a new slightly enlarged D–12A engine capable of 500 bhp, took first and second places in that year's Pulitzer race, the winner flying at a formidable 243 mph. This

FIGURE 34.—Curtiss CR-3 seaplane racer, 1923, powered by Curtiss D-12 engine. (Smithsonian photo A-4655F.)

event took place a few days after the Schneider Trophy victory. Third and fourth places were taken by two new Navy Wright fighters (at 230 mph) powered by improved Wright T–3 engines capable of 780 bhp on the test bench. All other finishers were powered by D–12 engines. This was the last time the Wright–T engine was used for racing. Henceforth it would be found, in derated form, only on flying boats and other heavy aircraft.

In a two-day contest between Navy Lieutenants Brow and Williams after the Pulitzer race, the world speed record was spectacularly boosted to 266.6 mph, thanks to the new R2 C–1 and the D–12A. This record was to stand unchallenged for more than a year.

The last of Kirkham's triplanes, the A–3326, was entered for the Liberty Engine Builders Trophy, which preceded the 1923 Pulitzer race by a few days. While running well in the race, the triplane's overextended CD–12 engine broke its crankshaft and was completely wrecked and caused the A–3326 to crash-land. The incident perhaps would have been forgotten had the Curtiss Company not found it necessary to issue a statement. The company was anxious to make clear that the engine had been an experimental unit, originally rated at 325 bhp and installed in the triplane for the race. Against the wishes of the company, the engine had been fitted with high-compression pistons and boosted to give 450 bhp at 2,200 rpm, the highest rating on record for a CD–12.

63

The crankshaft of that engine had not been drop-forged. It was made from a slab forging and did not have proper grain flow. There had been no time available to make proper forging dies and the disastrous result had been anticipated. After this race the last remaining triplane was scrapped. A page of colorful aviation history had been turned.

A correspondent of the leading French aviation paper *L'Aéronautique,* after having had a look at the Curtiss and Wright engines toward the end of 1923, found it strange that in France only the Hispano-Suiza firm was engaged in the manufacture of monoblock engines, "a form of construction that appears to be so much in vogue in America." It had not dawned upon him that what really had happened was that during the previous six years the Curtiss and the Wright engineers had been trying to "out-Hispano" each other, and the original Birkigt concept had been left far behind in the process.

It has been recorded that in 1920 and 1921 France had made little progress toward very high speeds, in spite of the introduction of a completely new and special airplane, the Nieuport Sesquiplan. This lack of progress should be blamed on the lack of research in aero engines and the inability of the French Hispano to develop more than about 330 bhp. As previously stated, it had a greater frontal area than the D–12. The Hispano-Suiza could be run at higher revolutions per minute, but here the propeller tip speed problem loomed dangerously near. Sadi-Lecointe had nearly lost his life in 1921 when a propeller burst at high speed.

The Americans, meanwhile, had jumped into the competition for engine and propeller progress with considerable dash, and their efforts were beginning to bear fruit. The critical period from 1919 to 1923 may be termed decisive for France's loss of top place in aviation design. The Curtiss Company enjoyed an immense advantage in that Kirkham had anticipated, in 1917, the horsepower requirements of five years later. Wright had done almost as well by refining the original 300-hp Hispano into a much superior engine.

The year 1923 had been one of glory for the D–12, and just before the year ended the Army's engineering division at McCook Field started to test that engine in earnest.

A D–12 was installed in a DH–4 (Project XP–277) for service tests that were conducted with success. And D–12 engine 125, AS–23–154, was set up for a 50-hour endurance test, running with high compression and at high speed—that is, an endurance test under racing conditions. The results of the test are described in McCook serial report 2348. With compression of 5.8:1, the average power developed during the 50 hours was 440 bhp at 2,170 rpm. Maximum rating during the first full-throttle half hour of each of the five ten-hour runs, as well as during the last hour of the test, averaged 468 bhp at 2,240 rpm, with an average fuel (50 percent benzol) consumption as low as 0.48 lb/hp/hr. Highest power developed was 475 bhp at 2,320 rpm, which may be taken as indicative of the power developed during the Schneider and Pulitzer races of 1923. This test, which lasted from 3 December 1923 until 12 February 1924, revealed the remaining weaknesses of the design. The splines of the vertical drive shaft were unsatisfactory, and three of these had to be replaced during the test. Also, the cylinder block was found to be too fragile below the top flange. After 35 hours the right block had to be replaced by one from another D–12, and at the end of the test the left block was beginning to leak.

The high-compression D–12 ran with Stromberg NA–Y5A carburetors, already standard, and Splitdorf magnetos. The originally fitted B.G. plugs had to be replaced during the endurance test by A.C. plugs because the B.G. units became too hot, causing pre-ignition.

After the final inspection the engine's major parts that had not given trouble during the power runs were found in good condition. The lessons of the high-compression endurance test were immediately put into practice. The vertical drive shafts were redesigned, and henceforth the cylinder blocks were cast from Duralumin and gave no more trouble.

The result of these improvements soon was making headlines. On 23 June 1924 Lieutenant Maughan began a dawn-to-dusk continental crossing in a PW–8—the fifth one produced—that had been equipped with one of the improved D–12 engines and the already obligatory Reed propeller (see Figure 35).

Maughan started from Mitchel Field, Long Island, New York, at 3 a.m. Eastern Standard Time. The D–12 ran beautifully, and the first lap of 590 miles was covered in four hours when Maughan landed at McCook Field, Dayton, Ohio. The second landing was made at the Municipal Flying Field, St. Joseph, Missouri, at 10:50 a.m. Central Standard Time, 30 minutes sooner than the year before. The third stop (not official) was at North Platte, Nebraska, where Maughan arrived at 1:30 p.m. Twenty minutes later he was off again for Cheyenne, Wyoming, the next official stop, where he arrived at 2:17 p.m. Mountain Time. Then came the worst part, the crossing of the Rocky Mountains; but the PW–8 surmounted every obstacle in its path without trouble and arrived at the next landing place, Saldura, Utah, at 5:20 p.m. Pacific Time. The last lap also was covered without incident, and Crissy Field at San Francisco was reached at 9:48 p.m. Pacific Time, still in daylight.

FIGURE 35.—Curtiss Pursuit PW-8, 1924. This plane, powered by a Curtiss D-12 engine and piloted by Lieutenant R. L. Maughan, flew the "Dawn to Dusk Flight" of 2,700 miles from New York to San Francisco in 21 hours and 48 minutes on 23 June 1924. (Smithsonian photo A-4655G.)

The entire flight had taken 21 hours 48 minutes, but actual flying time for the 2,645 miles covered was 18 hours 20 minutes. The average flying speed was over 156 mph. Compared to the 26 hours, nonstop, of the Liberty-powered T–2 of May 1923, the advance was indeed impressive.

Since Maughan had felt ill during some stretches of the flight in the previous year, presumably because of exhaust fumes, the 1924 PW–8 had been fitted with long exhaust pipes leading behind the cockpit. This is the only example known of a D–12-powered airplane being so modified.

A couple of months after the epoch-making dawn-to-dusk record, one of the new D–12 engines arrived at McCook Field for another endurance test. It was engine 93, AS 23–144, and it embodied all the improvements resulting from the experiences of all the previous Navy and Army tests: Duralumin cylinder blocks, on which the length of the end water-jacket upper bosses had been doubled; redesigned vertical drive shafts; new type short-skirt pistons; and steel-backed connecting rod and main bearings. The engine, running with low-compression pistons, was given what may be termed an all-out test at high crankshaft speeds—higher than that of any test of a Curtiss engine since the K–12.

This latest D–12 stood up magnificently to all that was demanded of it, and, according to McCook report 2428, it "operated remarkably

66

FIGURE 36.—Views of Curtiss D-12 engine, 375 hp, 1922.
(Smithsonian photos A-4655C, A-4655D.)

well without a single forced stop." All the tests—endurance, calibration, fuel consumption, and others—were effected between 30 September and 13 October 1924, a record low in test duration. The average maximum power developed was 444.5 bhp at 2,480 rpm, and, during a calibration run before the 50-hour test, 460 bhp at 2,490 rpm was reached, running on 40 percent benzol mixture. After the endurance test, the engine was stripped for a thorough inspection, as was customary. Apart from some warped exhaust valves, no fault could be found. Report 2428 concluded with the following statement: "The engine is a vast improvement over the original design." After this test, no more major design changes were to be effected, except the introduction of die-cast pistons with engine 138.

The normal rating, which had been raised from 375 hp at 2,000 rpm in 1922 (see Figure 36) to 420 hp at 2,200 rpm for the low-compression engine in 1924, was raised again to 435 hp at 2,300 rpm in 1925, beginning with the D–12C engines, the first of which was engine 253. The peak of the power curve was at 2,700 rpm, at which speed the low-compression model gave 466 bhp.

A high-compression model rated at 460 hp/2,300 rpm also was available, but lack of proper service fuel prevented its use in the United States. The low-compression service engine had no difficulty running on the

67

FIGURE 37.—Curtiss D-12D, 460 hp, 1927. (Smithsonian photo A-4666C.)

domestic aviation grade (D.A.G.) fuel of that time, which had an octane rating of about 50.

All later development was of minor importance and directed solely toward improving small details. In the following years, the original model was offered as the D–12C, and it was modified into the D–12D (see Figure 37) and the D–12E. Model D–12M was simply an older D–12 modified to the latest standards. The weight remained at 680 lb dry. Total installed weight, including radiator, piping, water, and oil, was slightly over 850 lb. On the later D–12 models, Scintilla magnetos (model AG–12D or VAG–12D) were increasingly used, and the Stromberg carburetor models advanced up to the NA–Y5F on the last engines.

The only disadvantages of the D–12 were in regard to maintenance. Spark plugs and carburetors were difficult to get at, and a whole cylinder block had to be removed in order to change a valve. McCook Field's engineers even were afraid that the maintenance problems were "somewhat beyond the capabilities of the average war-time station." This was an inevitable feature of the monoblock construction. When the first Hispano-Suizas appeared at the front in 1916 the French mechanics were not up to the task of maintenance. The entire program was in jeopardy, and the normal service use of the Hispano was delayed for six months at least. But the advantages of power, small size, and low weight were so exceptional that the disadvantages had to be accepted.

After 1925 the Curtiss Company stopped development on the D–12, and it then started to reap the fruits of the many years of effort that had gone into that engine. A virtual monopoly for fighter power plants had been reached and Kirkham's dreams had come true at last, though somewhat later than he would have foretold himself. Curtiss had now also secured an entry in air-cooled engine development by a low bid for the construction of three Army R–1454 radial engines, the cylinder development of which had been going on at McCook Field under S. D. Heron since 1920. The firm thus was able to look to the future with optimism and confidence. Orders poured in from the Army for D–12 engines to power the new PW–8 and PW–9 pursuits, and the Navy followed suit when naval versions of the two pursuits were adopted as the F6 C–1 and the FB–1.

In 1924, with the definitive establishment of the D–12 as a military engine, interest in racing (the peacetime substitue for war) appeared to be waning. The 1924 Pulitzer race at Dayton was a rather sad affair without much technical interest. The unassailable position of the D–12 was manifest, as all racers were so powered. The two R–6s and the winning R–3 monoplane had 500-hp D–12A engines. Indeed, this race was a retrogression compared to former events, as it had been decreed that the R–6 racers were to use wooden propellers. Reed's high-speed aluminum propeller was tragically vindicated, however, when Captain Skeel's Curtiss racer disintegrated in the air after his propeller burst while gathering speed in his starting dive. After this accident, the old-type wooden propellers were not heard of again, and the new metal propeller secured a position as impregnable as that of the D–12—a position crowned in 1926 by the presentation of the Robert J. Collier Trophy to Dr. Reed.

If the 1924 Pulitzer race had not been exciting, the Schneider Trophy race of that year was even less so, as it came to nothing. The American impact of 1923 had convinced the English and the Italians that a new approach was necessary.

The Italian authorities paid the D–12 the highest of compliments by decreeing that all their entries for 1924 were to be powered by the American engine, but since no aircraft was ready in time all foreign entries were withdrawn. The Americans then very sportingly declined to hold a contest that could only be a walkover. But this gesture would cost them the permanent possession of the Schneider Trophy. The United

FIGURE 38.—Curtiss V-1400, 500 hp, 1925. (Smithsonian photo A-4666D.)

States would have no difficulty in winning again in 1925 but there was to be no chance in 1926. Destiny must have had a hand in this because the gesture of 1924 would have a direct bearing on the British superiority during the Battle of Britain in 1940, as will be seen later.

One result of the crystallization of the D–12 design at Curtiss was that demands for more power, which inevitably were to be made, could be met only by enlarging the size of the cylinders in new models, without changing the basic design. We have already encountered the D–12A of 1923, which had had its bore increased by one-eighth inch and was able to develop about 500 bhp for racing. It was not rated for service, however, and only a few units were built. The design of a bigger engine, the V–1400 (see Figure 38) was started in 1924. It was introduced in the 1925 Pulitzer race, which it had no difficulty in winning, and it did not encounter any worthwhile opposition at the Schneider Trophy contest.

The V–1400 had its bore enlarged by another quarter inch (to 4⅞ in.) and its stroke also increased by a quarter inch (to 6¼ in.). This engine gave 620 bhp on the test bench, and it was even lighter than the D–12. The only departure from the basic D–12 design was the important one of using open-ended cylinder liners. The V–1400 passed a 50-hour test at 500 bhp in 1924 but it was not put into production. Twelve units were built, five of which were destined for the P–2 fighter.

70

FIGURE 39.—Curtiss PW-8 pursuit plane of 1924, powered by a turbosupercharged Curtiss D-12. (Smithsonian photo A-4667B.)

In 1925 another version appeared. This time, the bore was enlarged to 5⅛ in., with the stroke remaining at 6¼ in. This resulted in a swept volume of 1,570 cubic inches. The new engine, which later would become known as the Conqueror, appeared in time for the 1926 Schneider race but was not able to turn the scales in favor of the United States. Italy won. Development of the Conqueror continued slowly until 1933. The full history of these enlarged versions of the monoblock Curtiss design deserves special treatment and are not described here.

In the meantime, the engineering division at McCook Field was continuing experiments on the D–12, none of which became conclusive, mostly through lack of funds and the absence of interest at the Curtiss Company.

Early in 1923, preliminary steps had been taken to adopt the exhaust-driven turbosupercharger to the D–12. This type of supercharger resulted from a persistent American effort which had started in 1918 and about which the engineering division at McCook was still very eager. Thus, it was natural that when the first two Curtiss PW–8 fighters arrived at McCook Field for testing early in 1924, one (P–358) had a late-model General Electric turbo and a special propeller designed to give a maximum speed of 190 mph at 20,000 ft. During flight tests Lieutenant Macready flew the turbosupercharged PW–8 to 33,454 ft. (See Figure 39.)

Development on the turbo was slow, and it was 1926 before a PW–8

71

with a still newer type of ball-bearing turbo made a 220-mile cross-country flight at 20,000 ft. The distance was covered in 70 minutes at the estimated speed of 190 mph. A few Boeing PW–9 airplanes also were converted for turbosupercharging, and five Curtiss P–1C Hawks were turbo-fitted in 1927.

The flying tests of these airplanes evidenced a performance typical of all turbosupercharged engines: a certain sluggishness at take-off (due to the high exhaust back pressures generated at low altitudes) but a fine turn of speed at high altitude (166 mph at 25,888 ft) and the ceiling pushed upward by over 11,000 ft above that of the standard P–1. No further effort was expended on the D–12 turbo.

Early in 1924 Allison built a transmission that geared together two D–12 engines driving a single propeller. This 850-hp unit was tested with success but did not reach the stage of actual flight and no aircraft was designed around it. The idea was taken up by Lockheed Aircraft Corporation and the Menasco Manufacturing Company in 1937, and the result was the VEGA Starliner, which combined the streamlining of a single installation and the safety of a twin. During World War II Germany used coupled engines as a quick means of increasing power without designing new engines. The Mercedes DB 610 engines used in the Heinkel He 177a–3 and the Messerschmitt Me 261 are examples, but these remained experimental.

Because in 1923 the Liberty engine had for the first time run successfully as an inverted engine, the engineering division at McCook Field was keen to try the D–12 as an inverted engine. Special parts were built and installed, but the converted D–12 absolutely refused to operate in inverted position. Packard later was able to install an inverted 500-hp engine in a fighter (the Boeing XP–8) but without much success. The successful inverted fighter engine had to wait for the German engine manufacturers of World War II.

A mechanically driven centrifugal supercharger built by General Electric also was fitted to a D–12; thus the early Kirkham experiments of 1918 were taken up again. So fitted, the D–12 gave about 400 bhp at 19,000 ft. This combination was flight-tested in 1925 on the Army's DH–4B (Project XP–277) and on a Boeing PW–9 (P–356).

In mid-1925 the Army's engineering division renewed its attempts to secure more power from the D–12 engine. For this purpose an endurance test was started with an engine tuned to run at 2,800 rpm. After 17 hours the engine was disassembled and found in satisfactory condition. It then was reassembled and fitted with a low-altitude (7,500 ft) centrifugal supercharger. (See Figure 40.) Maximum power reached with the

FIGURE 40.—Curtiss D-12, 1925, with centrifugal supercharger.
(Smithsonian photo A-5235A.)

supercharger was 552 bhp at 2,800 rpm. The tests terminated because
of bearing trouble, but the high power and speed achieved were portents
of things to come. Finally, a Roots type supercharger, developed by
Curtiss, gave a theoretical power of 410 bhp at 5,000 ft but, although it
actually was fitted to a D–12, no practical work was done on it.

As a result of these experiments, a new—and the last—D–12 variant
would be introduced. This was the D–12F, which had a specially rein-
forced crankshaft capable of withstanding the higher loadings that resulted from supercharging the incoming explosive mixture. The military
designation for the D–12F was V–1150–7. These were the engines that
were fitted to the Curtiss P–5 fighters.

By 1925 the Curtiss model XPW–8B became the P–1 when fitted with
a D–12 engine and the P–2 with the V–1400 engine. These were the
first of a long pedigree of famous Hawk fighters that dominated the
1920s. The D–12 engine was so firmly established by now that it was
adopted for the Curtiss O–1 (Falcon) observation plane, instead of the
old Liberty, and this resulted in a saving in weight of 256 lb. The Falcon
became so fast and maneuverable that it was tested as a two-seat fighter,
which resulted in the A–3 attack plane of 1926.

73

From now on the D-12 service record becomes downright tedious; in fact, the only qualities by which the pilots of the later period still remember the D-12 are its dependability and lack of any kind of ill manners—a far cry from the temperamental K-12 of 1918 that started it all.

In 1927 the engine had reached that very high degree of reliability which in aero engine development may be considered synonymous with obsolescence. While new engine types were taking over the stage, the D-12 was mentioned only from time to time in some tale of dogged reliance, like the story of one that flew some time without water with no apparent ill effects. Another still more unbelievable story was of a pilot who saw his D-12 run to a seemingly impossible high speed by a maladjustment of the variable-pitch propeller. A connecting rod was broken in the process but the D-12 was able to continue at 1,800 rpm and to deposit pilot and airplane without a scratch 15 minutes after the breakage, although four more rods had gone in the meantime.

In July 1928, 19 Curtiss Hawk fighters made a flight from Selfridge Field, Detroit, to Kelly Field, Texas, covering 1,400 miles in 13 hours. They flew on schedule in perfect formation in poor weather without a single mechanical breakdown in any engine. Thus, it was without question that on 11 October of that year the D-12 received U.S. Government Approved Type Certificate No. 10 (approved for civil aviation use). In 1930 a flight of Hawks made a winter Arctic patrol of 3,500 miles. The airplanes were never under shelter but the engines gave no trouble.

A total of 1,192 D-12 units had been built during the active period 1922-1932. At Buffalo, 1,105 units were made up to 1931, and, after the merger with Wright, 87 more were built at Paterson, New Jersey— 15 in 1930, 70 in 1931, and the last two in 1932. The price of a standard D-12 during the 1920s was about $9,100, and the life between overhauls was about 200 hours. A last attempt was made in 1930 to introduce the D-12 as the power unit for the Curtiss XBT-4 trainer but nothing came of that. After 1930 the D-12s were rapidly replaced by engines of newer and different designs.

In any art that progresses so quickly as that of the aero engine, a monopoly of any kind can be held only for a short time unless all-out efforts incessantly are made to improve the product. In the case of the D-12, the Army's engineering division was undertaking more experimental work than the Curtiss Company, which was enjoying what seemed to be an unassailable position. But the efforts to unhinge the monopoly already were underway and their results soon were to be seen.

France, unhappy at having lost so many records to the D-12-powered airplanes, reacted at once. Marc Birkigt, Hispano-Suiza's chief designer, built two new 12-cylinder Hispano-Suiza engines. The first, designed in 1923, was a three-row, broad arrow, or W-type, engine made up of three blocks of the earlier 300-hp V-8 on one crankshaft. This engine was followed, in 1924, by a V-12 of the same cylinder dimensions but in two blocks of six. At the end of 1924 a special Bernard speedster—fitted with a carefully prepared three-row, 12-cylinder Hispano boosted to 600 bhp and with a Levasseur-Reed propeller—raised the world speed record to 278 mph. The Americans did not press the issue, and the French record, as a landplane record, would stand for eight years. Thereafter, until 1939, all absolute speed records would be established by seaplanes. Curtiss had missed an opportunity, as Hispano-Suiza had made its last effort. Apart from adding another 10 mm to the bore of its engines, Hispano-Suiza did not change the basic design and in 1928 it was still building the same kind of engines that it had in 1915.

The United States easily would have been able to beat the Bernard in 1925 with the Curtiss V–1400 engine. The latter had the same power as the record-breaking Hispano but it had a much smaller frontal area and was lighter by 200 lb.

No French airplane proved capable of beating the speed record over 100 km, which Lieutenant Cyrus Bettis, the Curtiss R3 C–1 racer, and the V–1400 engine established in the 1925 Pulitzer race—a record which stood for many years. But money was running short and experiments with the air-cooled radial were clearly favored. Besides, the Americans still had no desire to emulate the French racers and their very high landing speeds—the fiasco of the Wildcat in the Gordon Bennett race of 1920 still hurt.

The opposition in the United States against the D–12's supremacy was on a more ambitious scale and the principal agent here was the Navy, which was not happy with the state of affairs and had already tried on several occasions to back other promising-looking designs. First the Wright T–2 had been tried, and later a few Packard A–1500 engines had been installed in a later variant of the Boeing FB–1, neither with lasting success. What the Navy really wanted was a fighter with an adequate air-cooled engine, and it looked wistfully to England where all fighters were powered by air-cooled radials of about 400 hp and giving a very good account of themselves. In fact, the English would have been hard put to imagine how a real fighter could be powered in any other manner.

Contracts with Wright to develop successively the P–1 and P–2 radials were not proceeding fast enough for the Navy, and Wright's management was not very keen on speeding up the development of air-cooled engines at a time when its Hispano derivatives were already marvels of reliability—really a sign of obsolescence, as we have noted. Wright also put great hopes on its new T–2 engines, which were intended to replace the Hispano.

The overwhelming success of the D–12 and difficulties with the T–2 and, later, the T–3 engines, which did not live up to expectation, changed Wright's policy overnight. First, the company entered the air-cooled engine business in force by buying up the Lawrance Company, which was selling 200-hp radials to the Army and the Navy, especially to the latter. To get a new fighter engine quickly, Wright accepted a Navy proposal to scale down the 850-lb P–2 engine of 450 bhp to one of about 350 bhp in order to attain the 650-lb weight limit, the maximum with which light fighters for the Navy could cope.

Frederick Rentschler, Wright's energetic president and hitherto one of the staunchest believers in Wright's water-cooled engines, decided suddenly, in 1924, that the time for a change had come and, apparently not counting on the necessary backing from his board, resigned from the firm. His purpose was to give the Navy the engine it wanted, and perhaps even a better one. The decision had been reached in full agreement with and perhaps at the instigation of George Mead, Wright's chief engineer, and of his assistant Andrew Willgoos, the men who had been responsible for the excellence of the final Wright-Hispano development. They were convinced that the era of the air-cooled engine was at hand.

Rentschler lost no time in bringing his plans to fruition. He secured capital and plant space from the Pratt & Whitney Tool Company in Hartford, Connecticut, and made certain to obtain from the Navy a promise to back a superior radial engine if one could be made, a promise the Navy was eager to make. The story of the new enterprise has been told. Mead and Willgoos left Wright also, and in December 1925 the first Wasp was produced, exactly eight years after the first K–12 and still with the same power and the same dry weight.

The 9-cylinder Wasp, developing 425 bhp, weighed 650 lb, a difference in installed weight of some 200 lb in favor of the Wasp when compared to the D–12. The Wasp killed outright the new scaled-down Wright of 350 hp, and at the same time sounded the death knell of the D–12.

For carrier-based fighters the advantages of an air-cooled radial engine over a liquid-cooled engine were overriding: (1) less maintenance, (2) less vulnerability to battle damage, (3) inherent lightness, and (4) compactness. The weight-saving features of the short crankshaft and crankcase of the radial engine also permitted an increased rate of climb and a lower landing speed. The compactness of the radial made for a shorter air-craft, thereby allowing greater maneuverability in the air and for more planes to be accommodated on an aircraft carrier.

The result was that the Wasp was received enthusiastically. Further-more, a bigger model, the Hornet, which would compete with the most powerful existing water-cooled engines was nearing completion.

In 1927 the Wasp was mounted on the Wright Apache fighter that had been designed to receive the 350-hp Wright radial, and the Navy ran it through a series of flight tests in competition with a D–12-powered Curtiss F6 C–1 and with a Boeing FB–4 having a Packard A–1500 engine. The results were highly satisfactory to the Navy, as the new Wasp engine came up fully to expectations. Some time afterward the Wasp was put into an Army Curtiss Hawk pursuit plane (the XP–3) for another suc-cessful evaluation.

There is no doubt that the Pratt & Whitney Wasp was of first-class design. Its importance would become supreme not only as an engine for military planes but for commercial aircraft also. Obviously, the most important advantage of air-cooling was that neither radiator nor plumb-ing was needed, thus doing away with sources of frequently recurring trouble; also, the cylinders, being fitted radially around the crankcase, were very accessible and made for easier maintenance.

The lightness of the air-cooled power plant enabled the Wasp-Apache combination to establish a world altitude record. The Wasp's ascend-ancy over conventional (meaning D–12) engines was pushed home con-vincingly during maneuvers over the Panama Canal in 1929 when the carrier-based Boeing and Vought Corsair fighters were able to outclimb and outfight the older, liquid-cooled Army Hawks.

To the Navy's complacent, though premature, satisfaction, compara-tive flight tests in 1926 and 1927 showed that the maximum speed of the Wasp-powered Hawk fighter was not less than that of the D–12-powered model, which then appeared to lose some of the aura that hitherto had been associated with low frontal area. It was not clearly appreciated then, however, that this might be true for speeds like those of the Hawks, which were in the neighborhood of 160 mph and thus still at the level attained by Kirkham's two-seat fighters in 1918. The increase in resist-ance, as a result of a greater frontal area, was compensated for by lighter weight and a cleaner engine installation design. The results of the 1926 and 1927 tests were thought to be valid absolutely, and the lessons of Loening receded in the background, at least for American designers. These designers would be reminded of those lessons a few years later, when they would become aware of a completely opposite development that had occurred elsewhere.

Finally, at the end of the decade, a belated attempt was undertaken to challenge the air-cooled engine's position by a new approach toward a still smaller frontal area, coupled to a much-reduced weight of both coolant and radiator by the introduction of high-temperature cooling. Research on this "hot" cooling can be traced back to McCook Field as early as 1923. The coolant adopted was ethylene-glycol, in America known under the trade name Prestone.[3] Several Curtiss D–12 and Conqueror engines were converted to Prestone cooling during 1928 and 1929 and submitted to extensive tests, both at the Wright Field laboratory and, later, in the air.

One Curtiss P–1B Hawk was used with a radiator, the size of which had been reduced by 70 percent, and a P–1C Hawk was fitted with wing radiators. During the Cleveland aeronautical races of 1929, Lieutenant Doolittle put one of these fighters through its paces with an unforeseen result. The reduction in radiator size increased the diving speed to such an extent that the plane shed its wings when accelerating during an outside loop and Doolittle had to take to his parachute.

The engineering division at McCook Field had specified a coolant temperature in the radiator of 300° F. As a consequence, the cylinder-head temperature of the D–12 rose from 378° to 508° F and that of the barrel from 187° to 209° F. The aluminum block-cum-steel-barrel construction could not adapt to these temperature rises and the glycol began to seep into the crankcase at the lower joints between the barrel and the jacket. This difficulty and other troubles that developed were impossible to remedy on the existing design. The result was a difference in opinion between Curtiss and the Army's engineering division. The Curtiss engineers maintained that the tests showed clearly that the specification for 300° F was exaggerated, as the oil cooler was becoming bigger than the coolant radiator, which was true. To this, the engineering division retorted that the real trouble lay with the seven-year-old block design. This was true also, but the Army went further and expressed the conviction that all monoblock forms of construction were obsolete, and in this the Army would be proved wrong.

---

[3] Shortly after Prestone was introduced as an automobile antifreeze a rust inhibitor and a leak sealer were added to its ethylene-glycol base. It then became entirely unsuitable for use in aircraft engine cooling systems because the added chemicals would form a jelly-like substance if the solution became too hot—that is, at temperatures above 250° F. Some D–12 engines were ruined when an overzealous supply officer replaced glycol with Prestone in an emergency.

FIGURE 41.—Curtiss Chieftain, 600 hp, 1927. (Smithsonian photo A-4666.)

Although the application of high-temperature cooling to the D–12 was not conclusive and did nothing to keep that engine in the forefront, the data gathered were to be of great consequence for the future of high-performance fighter engines. It was with glycol also that the term "liquid cooling" came into use; hitherto, all service engines had been cooled by plain water.

The Army would remain adamant for several years in its attitude toward a 300° coolant temperature, though later experience and research would show that much better results could be achieved with the ultimately used temperatures of 250–265° F.

A result of the Army's position was the revival of the individual steel cylinder in the United States. Curtiss, for one, brought out in 1932 a so-constructed V-12 engine designed for 800–1,000 bhp and able

FIGURE 42.—Packard diesel DR-980, 225 hp, 1930. (Smithsonian photo A-4666B.)

to withstand cooling fluid temperatures of 300° F. The aluminum monoblock engine would nevertheless keep in the forefront, but it would no
longer be a Curtiss type.

At any rate, the water-cooled engine began fading away in the United
States after 1928. The Navy followed its decision, made public in 1927,
not to buy any more water-cooled engines, and, as a result, Curtiss was

driven to develop an air-cooled, hexagonal, 12-cylinder engine (Figure 41) with overhead camshafts. The company intended to marry the advantages of air-cooling to those of water-cooling. Packard went further by trying to lure the Wright Whirlwind customers away by producing, under heavy publicity, a Diesel air-cooled radial engine (Figure 42) of equal size and horsepower and—by means of some very clever technical tricks—with the same weight as the Whirlwind.[4] Both companies tried to force destiny by overstressing the technical possibilities of the moment.

In the meantime, the void in Wright's engineering department made by the leaving of Mead and Willgoos had been filled when S. D. Heron and E. T. Jones, hitherto working for the Army's engineering division, put their eminent talents at the firm's disposal in 1926, when McCook Field was abandoned for Wright-Patterson. Jones became Wright's chief engineer, while Heron continued his research at Wright Field. The efforts of these two men for the Wright Company soon brought fruit. Wright's water-cooled engines were abandoned and the Whirlwind was brought to J–5 status—the ultimate pitch of perfection—in 1927, permitting all the admirable ocean crossings and long-distance flights for which that year was to become so famous. The old Navy-Wright radial, the P–2 called the Cyclone, likewise was improved and developed to become one of America's leading air-cooled radials.

Neither the Curtiss Hexagon nor the Packard Diesel had become accepted, and after the Curtiss-Wright merger the emphasis of the company's engineering department was shifted to the Cyclone, while Packard stopped making aero engines altogether. Pratt & Whitney then became the leading manufacturer of large aircraft engines in the United States.

The National Air Races meanwhile had degenerated into "free for all" events in which military planes and pilots of both services were allowed to show their stamina. In 1928 an air-cooled engine won for the first time. In fact, all entries were Wasp-powered, and the newly introduced Boeing F4 B–4 achieved a mean speed of 172 mph. That speed was impressive for a fighter powered by a radial engine, but when it is compared with the Pulitzer Race speeds of 206 mph in 1922 or the almost 250 mph in 1925 it is clear that no real research on high-speed craft had been effected.

In 1929, first place, at 194.9 mph, went to a new, specially designed racer, the Travel Air Mystery fitted with one of the new 9-cylinder, J–6 series Wright Whirlwind radials that had been boosted to develop 400 bhp. A lone D–12-powered Curtiss Hawk F6 C–3 Navy Pursuit (A–7144)

[4] See Robert B. Meyer, "The First Airplane Diesel Engine: Packard Model DR-980 of 1928." *Smithsonian Annals of Flight*, vol. 1, no. 2, 1964.

achieved only fourth place in spite of Prestone cooling and small side radiators. The disadvantages of the air-cooled radial with respect to frontal area were lessened considerably by the introduction of the N.A.C.A. cowl, which insured a much better airflow and less turbulence.

Also in 1929, the Curtiss Marine Trophy race for seaplane fighters was won by a Wasp-powered Curtiss Navy fighter. In the previous year this race had been won by a D–12-powered plane, as was the last of these races, which was held in 1930. Air-cooled engines powered the winners in all major national races during the decade 1931–1940. They predominated in all other spheres of aeronautics and even beat the world landplane (though not the absolute) speed record several times, beginning in 1932 when Jimmy Doolittle achieved 300 mph to beat the 1924 mark of 278 mph established by the Bernard-Hispano-Suiza racer.

Strangely enough, but very significantly, the D–12, which to all intents and purposes was as good as forgotten after 1931, would stage a sensational comeback in the same application as that which had distinguished it at the first—a pure racing engine. It all came through the activity of Steve Wittman, a specialist airplane designer and racing pilot who had made a name for himself in the early 1930s with some delightful little racers powered by the Menasco in-line air-cooled engine, which was being pushed to the limit of what it could stand. These small racers were fast, but they were no match for the big radial-powered ships with engines of 800 hp or more. Wittman, around 1934, hit upon the idea of a perfect combination: a diminutive racer and a small engine that would be powerful enough to oppose the big Pratt & Whitney engine.

So it came about that Wittman designed the Bonzo, his masterpiece, around a secondhand D–12 engine he had purchased from an aircraft engine dealer in the East. Wittman had to take the D–12 as it was, without logbook or previous history; and he did not apply for help from Curtiss or from either of the armed services. The D–12 was thoroughly overhauled and tuned and then installed in the new Bonzo (Figure 43), surely the smallest and cleanest aircraft that a D–12 had ever pulled through the air.

The engine was first flown in its normal, water-cooled state, but Wittman soon decided that the D–12 would have to be converted to high-temperature cooling, as it was useless to install a small engine into a small fuselage if it had to carry a big, heavy radiator. Jimmy Doolittle was asked for his opinion about the conversion, and he advised against using glycol with a D–12, no doubt remembering the troubles that had been encountered during the years 1928–1930. Nevertheless, Wittman determined that he had to take the risk, and he set himself single-

FIGURE 43.—Steve Wittman's Bonzo racer, powered by a Curtiss D-12. (Photo courtesy of Experimental Aircraft Association. Smithsonian photo A-5083A.)

handedly to a task that had caused so many headaches to the Wright Field engineers some years earlier.

The major problem was in the devising of a proper seal for the lower end of the cylinder barrels, because, as in the Army experiments, the standard seal allowed the coolant to leak into the crankcase when the engine worked at high temperatures. Only after a considerable amount of experimental work were the problems that derived from high temperatures finally solved. A reduced Prestone radiator was positioned, most originally, inside the fuselage and directly in front of the engine. The cooling air entered through a duct in the propeller spinner and was scooped up by a fan turning in front of the radiator.

High-compression pistons giving a ratio of 8:1 were installed, and 100-octane gasoline was used. These modifications resulted in a "hot" engine. Power was estimated at 485–500 bhp and maximum revolution at around 2,550–2,600 rpm. The engine operated at coolant temperatures of between 275° and 325° F.

The first appearance of the Bonzo, in the 1935 Thompson Trophy race, saw the cooling troubles not completely cured, but nevertheless the plane achieved second place at 218 mph.

83

The big show came in 1937 when Wittman qualified his Bonzo at 275.6 mph. From the start of the race the Bonzo's supremacy was obvious, and for 17 laps the little jewel outpaced the field, which included three beasts powered by 1,000-hp Hornet sprint engines. The D–12 was showing the same supremacy over brute power that it had enjoyed 15 years earlier. But with victory in sight Wittman suddenly had to hold back because of lack of oil pressure. Bad luck had frustrated a fine performance. Early in the race, a bird, or a stone, had hit the propeller, throwing it slightly out of balance, and the resulting vibrations had broken an oil line.

TABLE 1.—*Progressive development of Curtiss monoblock engines from 1916 to 1929.*

Model	Year	Rated hp	RPM	Weight (lb)	Displacement (cu. in.)	Designer
AB	1916	300	2250	725	829	Kirkham
D-1200	1917	400	2500	625	1145	Kirkham
K-12	1918	375	2250	665	1145	Kirkham
C-12	1920	400	2250	675	1145	Porter
CD-12	1920	325	1800	704	1145	Nutt
CD-12A	1921	375	2000	704	1145	Nutt
D-12	1922	375	2000	671	1145	Nutt
D-12C	1925	435	2300	694	1145	Nutt
D-12D	1926	460	2300	680	1145	Nutt
D-12E	1927	435	2300	685	1145	Nutt
D-12*	1929	435	2300	685	1145	Nutt

NOTE: Copies of McCook Field reports on this series of engines are available from the National Air and Space Museum, Smithsonian Institution.

*Approved Type Certificate No. 10, United States Government, 1 March 1929.

In the 1938 Thompson Trophy race the Bonzo, with a leaking radiator, came in third. Time was definitely running out now for the D–12. In 1939, after further polishing, the Bonzo was able to attain 325 mph, but during the race Wittman was penalized a full lap for cutting inside a pylon and he could take no better than fifth place.

It was a pity that those last brave attempts of Wittman and the D–12 to show again the worth of low frontal area had been pursued by such continued bad luck. It was as if Fate would not tolerate such an old design to win races against all comers instead of peacefully retiring into its niche in history.

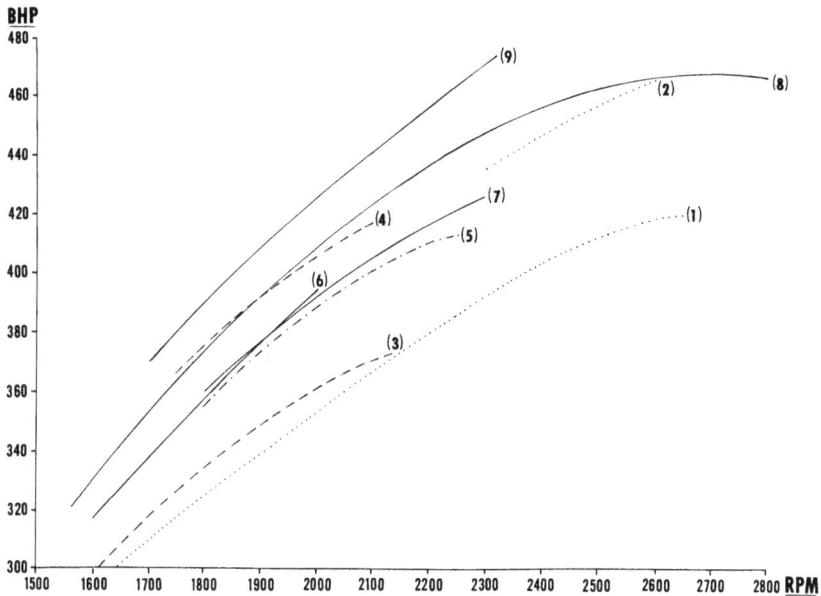

FIGURE 44.—Power curves of Curtiss 12-cylinder engines, 1918-1923. (1) Early K-12; compression ratio, 5.66:1. (2) K-12 No. 13 (height record engine), 11 January 1919; compression ratio, 6:1. (3) CD-12 No. 1, first Navy run, April 1921; compression ratio, 5.23:1. (4) CD-12 No. 3, 5 August 1921; compression ratio, 6.09:1 (50 percent benzol). (5) C-12 No. 1, 30 January 1920. (6) D-12 No. 1, Navy test, 9 July 1923; compression ratio, 5.3:1. (7) D-12 No. 22, 50-hour Army test, October 1923; compression ratio, 5.3:1. (8) Best power curve of a D-12 low-compression engine; compression ratio, 5.3:1. (9) D-12 No. 125, high-compression engine, tests of December 1923 through February 1924; compression ratio, 5.8:1.

According to Wittman, the engine in the Bonzo was sold during World War II and was used for testing propellers. The plane was preserved by the Experimental Aircraft Association, and it is on display in the association's museum.

Like many other reliable aero engines at the end of their flying careers, quite a few D–12s were converted for marine use. Some, no doubt, were used in rumrunners of the late 1920s, as boats so powered easily could outrun the more conservatively powered police patrol boats. Richard F. Hoyt, Curtiss Wright president, had a D–12 converted for use in a fast commuting boat of his. Several D–12 marine conversions were effected by Vimalert, a well-known Jersey City shop. One D–12 is at the Smithsonian Institution, one at the Air Force Museum in Dayton, Ohio, and one at the Musée de l'Air in Paris. It is hoped that a few others may be preserved, because the engine has a claim to such honor.

The Influence of the D-12

The story of the D-12 has ended, but the impact of its design on aero engine development starts a new tale that is equally interesting.

The central achievement of the D-12 may be taken as the winning of the 1923 Schneider Trophy. We have already seen that the surprise in European aviation circles had been great, and that this would be quickly followed by concrete forms of recognition.

The Italians were prompt to grasp the importance of the high-speed era that began with the D-12. While designs along similar lines were started in 1924 at the Fiat and Isotta-Fraschini works, the Italian Air Ministry decreed, as a stopgap, that all contenders for the 1924 Schneider race were to be powered by D-12 engines. At the same time it was hoped that for the 1925 race new 450-hp Fiats could be installed. These hopes did not materialize, and for the 1925 Schneider Trophy race Italy was represented by two Macchi flying boats powered by Curtiss D-12A engines of 500 hp. These entries had no chance against the new V-1400 engines that powered Doolittle's Army racer. In fact, one of the two D-12A engines refused to start.

It became obvious to the Italians that to install a foreign engine— which would of necessity always be last year's model—was not the way to win a race of such importance; so, the Italian engineers began to pro- duce their own compact high-power engines. The new engines did not follow the aluminum-block construction entirely. They had steel cylinders with welded-on, steel water jackets and so were more like the Napier Lion in form, but they were compact and highly efficient. The first to appear, the Fiat A-20, had cylinder dimensions much like those of the D-12 (115 by 150 mm) and it developed comparable power, with 410 bhp at 2,000 rpm. Of more importance was the A-24, a larger engine of 1,970 cubic inches that was being developed along parallel lines. The A.S.2, a racing version of the A-24 and capable of 880 bhp, was installed in 1926 in an advanced monoplane Macchi racer that was able to snatch the Schneider Trophy away from America at the last moment, as another win by America would have meant permanent possession of the trophy. It was really at the last moment, as the United States had been so kind, or perhaps so complacent, as to postpone the race for 16 days in order to enable the Fiat engines, which had suffered the inevitable last-minute troubles, to join the race. Considering this gesture, coupled with the fact that the United States graciously had canceled the 1924 race for lack of proper competition, it may be said that America had gone to great lengths in order *not* to retain the Schneider Trophy.

For the 1926 event the United States entered two 1925 Curtiss racers with new engines. One, powered by a Packard, was lost during preliminary trials; the other, powered by the first of the new Curtiss V–1550 monoblock engines, did not finish the race.

The 1926 Schneider Trophy race was a touch-and-go affair, as demonstrated by the fact that Italy tried in vain to obtain a postponement of that race to 1927. Another attempt to curb American engine superiority had been brought forward by France and Italy at a meeting of the Fédération Aéronautique Internationale (FAI) in 1925. It had been proposed that the Schneider Trophy competition be changed from a pure speed event to one for seagoing machines with a certain minimum useful load, a request that had been rejected by the FAI.

The concept of a small frontal area came back with the entry in the 1929 contest of a very small Fiat racer powered by a Fiat A.S.5 engine of about 1,000 bhp. For the 1931 race, Macchi-Castoldi prepared a racer that was powered by two such engines mounted in-line (known as the A.S.6), thus having the frontal area of only one engine. That seaplane racer was not ready in 1931 but it won the world's speed record in 1933 and again in 1934 with 443 mph, a speed that stood as a world record until 1939 and that still stands as a seaplane world record for piston engines.

Although the D–12 provided the basis for the development of the liquid-cooled engine in Italy, this was nothing compared to the enthralling story of how the British came to grips with the D–12 challenge and the advance in engineering that was spurred on as a result.

Again we must return to the 1923 Schneider Trophy contest. At Cowes, on that memorable September day, all who played a role in British aviation were present when the Supermarine-Napier was dethroned by the Curtiss in such an unmistakable manner. The impact of that exploit was accurately sensed by almost everyone.

One manufacturer, not content to ponder, decided to act swiftly. That manufacturer was Charles Richard (later Sir Richard) Fairey, at that time the head of England's largest aircraft factory. What his feelings were when confronted with the Curtiss racer and its D–12 are best expressed in a speech titled "American Aviation" that he gave at a Royal Aero Club dinner in November 1925. Following are excerpts from that speech as paraphrased in an article in *Flight* magazine (3 December 1925, p. 794):

In Europe [just prior to 1923] the position was that French and British aircraft designers were limited by the large cross-sectional area of their fuselages, by projections of various kinds, by exposed radiators and by wooden propellers, which had about reached their limit as regards tip speeds.... Then arrived in this country, in 1923, the American Schneider Cup machines. He [Fairey] had been among those privileged to examine the American machines and engines at Cowes, and very quickly realised that here new brains had been at work. The exposed radiators disappeared and had been replaced by wing surface radiators. The old wooden propellers... had given way to all-metal propellers of thin section, running at tip speeds hitherto considered impossible and giving efficiencies in excess of 80 per cent.... The Curtis D.12 engines were of narrow Vee form, and enabled the fuselage cross-section to be reduced to the minimum which would accommodate the pilot and the fuel.

... Mr. Fairey stated that there had been no revolutionary change in design. It was all a matter of recognising their old friend (or enemy) KSV2.... It came down to this, then, that the reason for the present American superiority was that American designers had recognised this fundamental law, while European designers had not, or had failed to heed it.

While Loening's admonitions of 1919 and 1920 were sinking into oblivion in the United States, they were now being discovered by the English.

There was a reason for Fairey's heightened sensitivity to the racy lines of the Curtiss. It came from the frustrations he had undergone with his Fairey Fawn, a two-seat bomber brought out in 1922 in accordance with an Air Ministry specification (No. 5/21). The civil servants at the Air Ministry had interfered with the original design in their own way, imposing modifications and additions that officially were meant to follow all kinds of safety rules, but the result was that the Fawn became a sorry-looking craft. Although powered by a 450-hp Napier Lion, it was barely able to make more than 100 mph, while in squadron service the fastest speed it attained was about 90 mph. In spite of all this, the Fawn, as a new type, came on the secret list.

The D–12 gave Fairey the inspiration he was waiting for, and he arranged for an early trip to the United States. He visited the Curtiss works and after a short but fruitful meeting was on his way home with a license to build the D–12 and Reed propeller in his pocket and a complete D–12 in his stateroom. He did not trust that mechanical jewel out of his sight. There was a strike in progress when the ship docked, but he managed to smuggle the engine ashore, firmly resolved that soon more would be heard from it, and from him.

The news of the Fairey-Curtiss arrangements was first mentioned and benevolently commented upon by C. G. Grey in an editorial of 5 March 1924 in his magazine *The Aeroplane*. The American press received the announcement with delight. The following month's issue of the *United States Air Service* contained a short comment by a staff writer which, in

FIGURE 45.—Fairey Fox bomber, 1926, powered by a Curtiss D-12. (Smithsonian photo A-4667.)

the light of what was to follow, put its author among the few true prophets in the history of journalism. "We are inclined to wish [the British] every success in their use of American ideas and it is not improbable that, with the ample resources behind the British Aircraft industry, substantial improvements along lines originally developed in this country may ensue." And that was exactly what was going to happen, but only after much ballyhoo.

Fairey's goal was simple. He wanted a new airplane, built closely around the D–12, to set an example of what his own vision, unhampered by bureaucratic intervention, could accomplish. In those days aircraft were built quickly, and the new Fairey Fox (Figure 45), a bomber, started its maiden flight on 3 January 1925.

The Fox was an uncommonly beautiful airplane, shaped like an arrow and making thorough use of combining streamlined form with the small shape allowed by the D–12 and the Reed propeller. The first flight was made with wing radiators, but since these were unable to cool the engine sufficiently a retractable ventral radiator was added. The oil was cooled without any increase in drag by making the bottom of the oil tank form part of the fairing beneath the engine. Fairey and his design staff had further provided that all equipment, when not in use, could be

89

stowed inside the fuselage. This was not the case in contemporary airplanes, which often were loaded with miscellaneous gear hung externally.

A special gun mounting for the rear gunner-bombardier was a great improvement over the earlier used ring. When not in use the gun could be stowed within the top fairing of the fuselage and still remain available for instant use; and it could be so operated that in most attitudes the gunner was sheltered by the windscreen, a most necessary protection when flying at·speeds in excess of 140 mph. The new mounting also made it possible to obtain certain fields of fire—such as vertical downward over the side—which were not easily obtained with the ring mounting. The pilot-operated gun was inside the fuselage, and a trap in the floor was opened for bombing. The fuselage was of small frontal area, and the wing section had minimum drag. Special care was taken to place the wings in relation to the body in such a manner that the greatest aerodynamic efficiency was obtained.

The results fully justified Fairey's foresight. With the same bomb load as the Fawn, the Fox reached a maximum speed of 156.6 mph, which was greater than any contemporary British fighter could muster. The Fox created an immediate stir in military aviation circles, and when the plane was shown to Air Marshall Sir Hugh Trenchard on 28 July 1925 a complete squadron was ordered on the spot. Consequently, the government officials were forced, grudgingly, to issue a specification (21/25) for an aircraft that had been designed in defiance of all existing specifications. For this violation of the sacrosanct rules of bureaucracy Fairey would not be forgiven, as he soon would find out.

One of Fairey's immediate plans was to build a factory in England for the production of the D-12, which he had renamed the Fairey Felix. The new factory would enable him to fill the orders that he was convinced soon would be streaming in. He also was building a single-seat fighter, the Fairey Firefly, around the D-12. It was designed to outfly anything extant, including the Fox itself, with a maximum speed of 188 mph. The position of Fairey's new airplanes appeared to be practically unassailable.

In its issue of 24 April the publication *Flight*, which more or less presented official thought to the public, had commented praisingly on the D-12 and on the licenses Fairey had secured; and the publication's special British industry number of May 29 had pictured the D-12—as the Fairey Felix and rated at 415 bhp at 2,000 rpm and 470 bhp at 2,300 rpm—amidst all the familiar British engines. But a year later, with the appearance of the Fox, the flouting of Air Ministry rules, and the ordering of an entire squadron in a highly irregular manner, a reaction began and attempts were made to belittle the D–12. Thus, an editorial in the 12 November 1925 issue of *Flight* that was tendentiously headed "Is It Cricket?" deplored the "official acquisition of a batch of American engines in a certain new type of British aeroplane"—the more so because the acquisition was made "without stipulation that the type tests in force must be passed though it is proposed to put one of the engines through the tests, there is no obligation to do so or attached thereto." The point was clear: "Why," asked the British aero engine manufacturers, "are our products to be subjected to a very severe acceptance test [and severe it was] when the first foreign engine that one of our aircraft manufacturers fancies is bought in quantity without more ado?" But here *Flight* had been wrong. There very positively had been attached an obligation for the D–12 to pass the official British type test. So, in the following week there appeared a second editorial titled "The Other Side" in which it was explained that

There was hurry because the engines were ordered for a test squadron and it would not have been advisable to wait for the passing of the engine test, and as the engines had passed the equivalent test in America they were ordered, but the Company has undertaken to pass the test as soon as possible and before the machines are delivered to the Service. Concerning the decision to order a fairly large quantity of D-12 engines, it may be said that the entire design of the Fox was based on the use of the D-12 engine.... Any further engines of the type are to be manufactured in this country when they will of course, be entirely British, except for the original design.

The second editorial, which clearly had been inspired, or written, by Fairey himself, made it quite clear for the first time that the heart of the matter was the D–12 itself and not the manufacturer's fancy.

Appearing in the same issue of *Flight* was a letter from Geoffrey de Holden Stone, a well-known aeronautical writer, in defense of Fairey and his Felix engine: "Be British or Buy British is quite admirable as a policy . . . if possible. . . . Without mentioning names, among British engines we have two makes of radials, of some 3 ft 9 to 4 ft diameter and one broad arrow model of the same width, each of the type the world's best and all alike available to Mr. Fairey had they suited his purpose, clearly then, they did not."

Other letters came in. One pointed to the fact that the purchase of 30 D–12 engines would cost the taxpayer 60,000 pounds sterling, and another let it be known that there already was heard a "demand for a second service squadron for the testing of another new aeroplane with a foreign engine," alluding, no doubt, to the single-seat Firefly. The refusal of one D–12 to spring to life on an Italian racer at the 1925 Schneider Trophy contest was also given more publicity than it was worth.

91

The issue was even brought before Parliament during the November 18 session when Rear Admiral Murray Sueter asked the Secretary of State for Air, Sir Samuel Hoare, why Fairey had to install the D–12 engine. The Secretary's answer was short and concise: "There was no other engine available."

The first attempt for the D–12 to pass the official British type test was made around November 1925 in accordance with British Test Schedule No. 4, which had come in force a few months earlier. The 100-hour test called for ten 10-hour runs at 90 percent of full power and at normal revolutions. At the end of each 10-hour run the engine was to be opened up to full throttle (meaning take-off condition) for the last five minutes, and the horsepower rating so obtained for the five minutes would have to be not less than rated full power. This was a very tough test and not many engines had passed it up to that time. In this case, the matter was made more difficult by Fairey himself. He insisted on using the high-compression version, giving 470 bhp at full throttle and normal (2,300) revolutions because he needed every available horse for his purpose.

A specially prepared D–12 had been despatched by Curtiss to Farnborough, and at first it appeared that there would not be any difficulty, as the engine ran beautifully for the first seven runs. After 87 hours, however, a small screw in the oil pump worked loose and interfered with the oil circulation so that the test had to be terminated, in accordance with the rules. This, of course, was fuel for the fire of the D–12's opponents, and in the Parliament session of 25 November Colonel Woodcock raised some questions on the engine's test. Sir Samuel replied truthfully that the D–12 had failed in a duration test after 78 hours[5] and that, as a result, "certain modifications have been incorporated in the thirty engines on order."

The failure of the D–12 to pass its type test put Fairey in a quandary. He immediately cabled the Curtiss Company, urging that matters be put right at once, as the deliveries of the Fox were already scheduled for 1926. The Curtiss Company, firmly engaged on American Army and Navy orders and unable to ship another engine immediately, suggested that a stock production engine, out of the batch already received in England, should be presented. There was no alternative but to follow that suggestion. The second test was then passed without trouble except that after 92½ hours there was another small defect in the oil pump,

---

[5] It has not been possible to find out whether the engine failed after 78 hours or 87 hours.

but that defect was repaired at once and the remaining hours were run without mishap.

There were no more obstacles, and the Foxes were delivered in 1926 to No. 12 Bombing Squadron, which hitherto had been using Fawns. The new bomber was enthusiastically received, and it created a big impression at the R.A.F. Display in Hendon that same year. It would make itself even more strongly heard during the 1928 Air Exercises when the Fox squadron was able to elude all fighter opposition. For example, the official communique of 14 August 1928 stated: 'The most interesting feature of this evening's operations was an attempt to intercept the fast Fox bombers, but once more the Foxes escaped, thanks to their great speed." Most comments dwelt on the need to concentrate on the development of faster fighters.

Meanwhile, British airplane manufacturers had not been content to sit idle and watch. At an early date they had started some very positive moves to counter the threat raised by the D–12 and the Fox. In the November 1925 session of Parliament, Lieutenant Commander Kenworthy had asked whether the whole affair was an attempt to break the monoply that had practically existed for 450-hp engines, upon which Sir Samuel Hoare had laconically answered "No, sir." That a de facto monoply existed could hardly be denied. It was enjoyed by the Napier Lion engine. Fairey had alluded to that engine in his Aero Club speech (referred to above) when he remarked: "The Napier is an excellent engine, except just for that one fundamental law of frontal area."

The Napier Lion had been designed in 1916 by Arthur John Rowledge in response to a government specification calling for a high-power altitude engine. The Royal Aircraft Factory, to whose designs the Napiers then were being built, suggested putting three of the already proven Hispano blocks on one crankcase. Considerations of frontal area played a very minor role in evaluating how the cylinders of an aero engine should be arranged. The Royal Aircraft project was a so-called "broad-arrow" or W design, where the cylinders are diposed in three rows of four, with the central row vertical and the two lateral rows inclined at an angle of 60° from the central row. So arranged, the three Hispano blocks would be able to give a maximum of about 300 hp.

Rowledge accepted the suggestion, but he enlarged the cylinder dimensions appreciably to a high-compression design of 12 cylinders, in the W arrangement, and 1,461 cubic inches displacement (28 percent more than the K–12). He used four valves per cylinder and two overhead camshafts, but otherwise he used the same closed-end steel barrel and aluminum monoblock construction as the Hispano-Suiza.

Rowledge, however, did not insist very long on following the Hispano lead, or even in trying to out-do it, as Kirkham would intend. He realized at an early stage that if reliability were to be achieved quickly, or at all, he would have to do away with the dry-sleeve Hispano construction and to tone down the monoblock tune a bit. The design was then changed, toward the end of the war, to one where the cylinder heads only were monoblock aluminum castings while the steel cylinders were separately fixed to the crankcase, each having its own steel cooling-water jacket. The Lion thus became a hybrid between the Hispano and Mercedes constructions. It was ready for service in 1919 and passed a 50-hour test in 1920 at a rating of 450 bhp. This came at a time when the Curtiss engineers were still struggling with the K–12 and, indeed, were about to abandon the project entirely.

The end of the war brought a sudden end to high-pressure research on new engines. The Napier management decided on a course of ever-increasing robustness and reliability for the Lion engine without changing the basic design. This policy carried the company into a leading position among the manufacturers of water-cooled engines in Great Britain.

Rowledge resigned from Napier in 1921 and joined Rolls-Royce, and the Lion then came under the responsibility of G. S. Wilkinson. By 1922 the Napier Lion was obtaining a reliability that left everything else in shadow, and it was the only engine suitable for use in single-engine commercial aircraft. The engine went from large overhaul periods to still larger ones, with big sales and nice dividends accruing from this situation. Reliability in aero engines was an extremely good thing at such a time, when it still was not taken for granted. Although Napier was on the crest of the wave of success, it did not realize that extensive research toward an eventual replacement is a necessity for survival. So it happened that in 1924 the Lion suddenly was confronted with the D–12, which, through prolonged development and research, had arrived at a more advanced position in aero engine technology.

It became painfully clear that the broad-arrow configuration, although advantageous for stiffness of crankshaft and rigidity of construction, was not very successful from the aspect of aerodynamic penetration. It was now obvious that the Napier Lion was the dominant cause of the unesthetic appearance of many postwar British airplanes fitted with water-cooled motors. Many such aircraft were characterized by very nondescript noses, and some were real plug-uglies. The Fairey Fawn was no exception.

Overnight, the D–12-powered Curtiss racers of 1923 and the Fairey

Fox made the British aircraft industry exceedingly nose-conscious. Designers at Napier were compelled to apply the necessary measures for the demanded beauty treatments toward refined aerodynamic entry or face the loss of many important customers. They thought at first that it was perhaps only a question of close-cowling the engine and putting a nice spinner in front. The first move was to cowl-in the engine as tightly as possible and to follow the lead taken by the Reed airscrew (in England to become the Fairey Reed) by removing the reduction gear, although this accessory had been a feature of the quick-running Lion from its inception. The loss of this gearing may not have been much bewailed, because in the same year Norman MacMillan's attempt at a round-the-world flight had been twice thwarted through the failure of the Lion's reduction gears.

At the end of 1924 the Lion VI was ready. It was the first model with direct-drive propeller and increased power rating. Also, for the first time the Lion was fitted to a single-seat fighter, the Gloster Gorcock. But these improvements were not enough. The second move was to clean up the space between the cylinder blocks, hitherto lazily filled with pipes, tubes, and rods. The pipes were neatly concealed within the blocks, and all the rest, including the carburetors, were moved to the rear and out of the way. These cleaned-up engines became the Lion VII and Lion VIII.

The Lion VII, developed especially for racing, was intended to power the next British Schneider Trophy challengers then in the works at Gloster and Supermarine. The Supermarine would finally bring the long-coveted trophy back to Britain in 1927 after a hotly contested race, at Venice, in which all the Italian engines had blown up. The Napier firm stated that its later Lion VII engine had a frontal area more than 2½ square feet less than that of the Lion V of the pre-D–12 era.

Mark VIII was the service version of the new Lion engine. Two fighters were designed around it—a new version of the Gloster Gorcock and the Avro Avenger—both of which sported finely streamlined noses that showed only two bulges at the sides where the cylinder blocks were in the way. These aircraft were of more pleasing appearance than any previous airplane powered by a Lion engine.

There was a similar development at the Rolls-Royce Company, which brought out a modified Condor engine, the Condor IV, also with a direct-drive Reed propeller. This engine was installed, and rather tightly so, in a Hawker fighter named the Hornbill. The tight cowling of such a huge engine resulted in a fighter of somewhat queer appearance that, though fast (190 mph), was unsuccessful for several reasons—

one being that the Condor, developing 700 bhp at 2,100 rpm, was not really suitable as a fighter engine.

Vickers resorted to another strategem by importing a French Hispano-Suiza V–12 of 400 hp and neatly fitting it to the company's newest fighter model. The manufacturers of air-cooled engines also were stirring, of course. The most aggressive of them all, Bristol—which manufactured the Jupiter air-cooled radial, of great reliability but of gigantic frontal area—at once started upon the design of a small-diameter radial, the Mercury, which for many years would try to hold fighter development committed to the radial engine.

When these attempts at close cowling of existing designs proved inconclusive, it appeared again that the D–12 really would remain unopposed and that Fairey might well get away with his scheme to build, in England, the Felix engine as the power plant for many squadrons of his advanced planes. But in this he was badly mistaken.

The responsibile directors at the Air Ministry had already taken the correct and destiny-shaping decision that what Britain really needed to remain in the forefront in aero engine progress was not an imported American engine, however epoch-making, and still less a rejuvenated British wartime design. Neither did they want to add a fifth manufacturer to the big four who already were hard pressed to live on the small orders then forthcoming. What was needed, they decided, was a new engine to be built by one of the established manufacturers along the lines of the D–12 but able to outperform it.

This policy was the responsibility of Lieutenant Colonel L. F. Rudston Fell, to whose insight and perspicacity Great Britain owes more than is commonly known. Fell was then assistant director for engine research and design at the Air Ministry. After evaluating the Fairey Fox and the Curtiss D–12 he sought to stimulate a leading engine manufacturer to develop an aero engine that could challenge the D–12.

The Napier Company was approached first because it was directly involved, having its bread-and-butter product in the same horsepower class. Fell suggested that Napier turn its broad-arrow W-12 into a narrower V-12 as an easy way out—in other words, a V-12-type Lion. But Napier turned down the offer, as it still had great confidence in the Lion. Also, the company was becoming less and less satisfied with big aluminum castings because of continually recurrent cracks in the monoblock cylinder head of the Lion; indeed, it was actually experimenting with a new design of a V-12 engine with individual all-steel cylinders, which appeared to give greater promise for reliable high power. Thus, it was moving a step away from the aluminum monoblock conception, taking the same road as the Curtiss Company would follow, around 1931, with its new 1,000-hp engine (the V–1800, already referred to) that would be built to withstand coolant temperatures of 300°F.

The new Napier engine with individual cylinders was not more successful than the Curtiss was to become. The result was that after the inevitable demise of the Lion, around 1930, the firm's sales declined rapidly and the company began looking eagerly for modern designs that would restore Napier to its former status. Eventually it began to experiment with new designs that were more audacious and complex than the monoblock construction had been.

After Napier refused to develop the desired engine, Colonel Fell made the offer to Rolls-Royce. Here he met with immediate approval. Henry Royce and Arthur Rowledge had, early in 1925, already started with the construction of an experimental monoblock engine of 16 cylinders in four blocks arranged in an X pattern. They were quite willing, however, to discontinue their not very conclusive experiments and concentrate upon the 12-cylinder engine proposed by the Air Ministry.

The new project was started in July 1925, the same month that Marshall Trenchard ordered his squadron of Fox bombers. Development of the new Rolls-Royce design was entrusted to Rowledge, who thus became responsible for creating a competitor for his own brainchild, the Lion. To make sure that there would be no mistake as to what the Air Ministry wanted, a complete D–12 was loaned to Rolls-Royce. Following the new classical lines of low frontal area and overall compactness, the design of a new aluminum monoblock V-12 that would supplant the D–12 took shape quickly. The prototype appeared in March 1926.

The first version of the new engine had dry cylinder liners and a supercharger, following the design of the earlier 16-cylinder "X" prototype of 1925. This construction was quickly abandoned because of the unreliability of the cylinder liner and cylinder head combination and also because of excessive frontal area. Other troubles developed, so Rolls-Royce changed to a construction having wet cylinder liners, as on the D–12, and dropped the supercharger temporarily. It had become evident that development of the supercharger would take time, and it was entrusted to a separate section of the company under the direction of J. E. Ellor.

At first the new design was known as the Rolls-Royce Falcon X, continuing a nomenclature started during World War I; but, as there was no similarity to the earlier Falcons, that name was soon dropped. The new model was to be known simply as the F-X until a better name was found.

97

When the first photographs of the F-X were released to the press in 1928, *Flight* uttered a famous last word, sounding ingenuous now but perfectly logical at the time: "One would not recognize the engine as a Rolls-Royce." It would not take very long before this kind of engine would be recognized everywhere as a typical Rolls-Royce, and its Curtiss ancestry would be completely forgotten. It should not be construed that Rolls-Royce actually copied the D–12; in fact, the only accessory that was kept more or less unchanged was the oil pump. The F-X engine was an entirely new project, starting where the D–12 had left off.

The cylinders, measuring 5 by 5½ in., displaced 1,210 cubic inches, or about 13 percent more than the D–12, and the engine was proportionately heavier. Adopting the now-classical monoblock construction, the cylinders consisted of steel barrels fitted into blocks made of a special aluminum alloy, of which Rolls-Royce, under the trademark "RR," and Devereux, as "Hiduminium," would bring out ever-improved alloys in the years to come. The steel barrels were open at the top, unlike the original Hispano and unlike the D–12 layout. This form of construction had been in use since the Wright T–2 and the Curtiss V–1400 of 1923–1924. It was first introduced by F. R. Smith on the aluminum-block Siddeley Puma engine of World War I.

One important divergence from the D–12 construction was that the cylinder heads and the induction-plus-exhaust passages were cast integral with the block. This was the exact opposite of the original K–12 idea where, it will be remembered, the cylinder block was cast integral with the crankcase while the cylinder head consisted of a separate casting. The K–12-type construction had now turned half circle; strangely enough, before long it would complete the circle and come back to the starting point, as it were.

The valves, four per cylinder, were actuated by a single overhead camshaft through rockers, and the whole distribution mechanism was enclosed in an oiltight cover lubricated by engine cranckcase oil, as had already become conventional in aluminum-block engines.

The year 1927 was spent in testing, modifying, and improving. In May or June of that year the first model completed a 100-hour endurance test with a rating of about 450 bhp at 2,100 rpm. The flight testing was undertaken, logically enough, on a Fairey Fox.

Meanwhile, in May 1926, the Air Ministry had issued specification 12/26, calling for a new plane to accommodate the forthcoming new engine. The Air Ministry had specified a two-seat, high-performance day bomber with a maximum speed of 160 mph—a performance which a year earlier would have been considered impossible, if not preposterous, had it not already been realized by the pace-setting Fox. Several firms, notably Hawker and Avro, set out immediately to design an aircraft that would meet the specification, and they were given every opportunity to work in close collaboration with the Rolls-Royce engineering staff. As a result, the Hawker product was offered as early as December 1926.

The new Hawker day-bomber, to become famous as the Hart, made its first flight in June 1928. Thanks to the low frontal area and high power of the newer, geared Rolls-Royce F-XI engine, the Hart made its debut with a sensational 180-mph maximum speed. This performance was better than any that could be achieved by a single-seat fighter, including the latest Bristol Bulldog that was just coming into service. It was a repeat performance of the Curtiss Triplane and Fairey Fox hits, but this time with a new actor who was not to leave the stage.

The Fairey Company had been "forgotten" on the list of firms invited to tender on specification 12/26. When Fairey heard of his exclusion he protested to Sir Hugh Trenchard, who immediately intervened so that Fairey also was asked to tender; but it was too late. The Fairey Fox II was ready in time, but its rivals, the Hawker Hart and the Avro Antelope, had come abreast of the technical advance that Fairey had achieved in 1925.

Although the Rolls-Royce-powered Fox II proved the faster aircraft, the Hawker Hart was chosen for production because of a technical advantage. The built-up construction of the Hart provided easier maintenance than the welded construction of the Fox, but Fairey felt that this was merely a trivial excuse for the ostracism which he was to suffer. Fairey remained convinced that he never was forgiven for having thrown the D-12 into the tranquil British manufacturer's family pool in 1925, even if the ripples it created were to be highly beneficial to England and British aviation.

In 1930 the Hawker Hart, an outstandingly fine aircraft, entered service with No. 33 Bomber Squadron. By the same year, the Foxes of No. 12 Bomber Squadron had been repowered with Rolls-Royce units, becoming model 1–A Foxes in the process. No D-12 was to be ordered again, and none was ever built in Great Britain. Nor was the order for Foxes repeated, except for some odd aircraft. After 1931, No. 12 Bomber Squadron, which had been equipped with Fairey Foxes since 1922, was progressively reequipped with Hawker Harts.

As a result of the Rolls-Royce efforts during the 1930 exercises, there were now two bomber squadrons able to evade the opposing fighters, and *Flight* observed dryly: "The manoeuvers emphasize the need of high performance in our fighter aeroplanes."

The reason for the absence of liquid-cooled engines on fighter aircraft as late as 1930 was not fortuitous, and neither was the fact that the Fairey Fox had been designed as a day-bomber and not as a high-speed fighter. This was the continuance of a policy dating from World War I when it was firmly believed that single-engine bombers should have the heavy, but reliable, water-cooled engines while the more agile fighters (or interceptors, as they later came to be called) were to be powered by the light and stubby air-cooled radials. The latter had great maneuverability and climbing power, virtues which were regarded as paramount in an intercepting fighter. As a further result, the bombers, because of sheer conservatism, remained needlessly slow and cumbersome.

There was another reason for the absence of liquid-cooled engines on fighter planes. In the development of the air-cooled radial, Britain was leading the world by a wide margin, with the result that this type of engine had been fostered as the power plant for fighter aircraft with a continuity that by 1925 had already grown into a tradition. The fact that in America the Curtiss D–12 was then the leading fighter, or pursuit, engine was not due to any clear-cut policy contrary to the British one; rather, it stemmed more from the obvious standing of the D–12, which simply had no competitor. The large air-cooled radial was not used in the United States before 1926 because there was no such engine available that could rival or even approach the triumphant D–12. We have seen that when the Pratt & Whitney Wasp arrived it was welcomed with open arms; indeed, it caused the downfall of the D–12 as soon as it was ready for service.

The first warning of a change in England came with the Fairey Fox and its judicious use of the compactness of the D–12, so much so that the air-cooled fighters after 1926 suddenly were found to be in a tight spot. It no longer made sense for an interceptor to twist itself ever so gracefully through the air when the bomber got through simply by flying straight on. Fairey himself had foreseen this situation. In 1926 he brought out the D–12-powered Firefly single-seater, the logical opponent for the Fox. He did not reckon, however, with official stubbornness.

Gloster and Avro were no luckier when they offered their Napier-engined fighters. Such fighters were not considered suitable by the Air Ministry, which issued its specification 12/26 around the new Rolls-Royce engine for a high-performance day-bomber with the idea of creating a rival for the Fox and not of obtaining a high-speed fighter.

Specifications 9/26 and 20/27 for fighters showed a determination on the part of the Air Ministry to stir the manufacturers into producing air-cooled, radial-powered craft that would become a match for the fast bombers. Specification 9/26 brought forth the 174-mph Bristol Bulldog, which was quickly put into production. Specification 20/27 called for a still faster fighter, capable of intercepting an enemy bomber passing overhead at 20,000 feet and flying at 150 mph. Air-cooled engines would be favored, and quite a few bids were handed in for interceptors capable of as much as 190 mph.

These endeavors to maintain a policy in favor of air-cooled engines were to be knocked down by the Rolls-Royce engine itself, which, in contradistinction to the D–12, progressed at a rate that can only be described as furious. There was no war being waged, and none was in sight. Thus, the reasons for these extraordinary exertions are worth closer scrutiny.

The underlying motive for the haste was undoubtedly the instinctive realization that the high state of perfection the air-cooled engine began reaching after 1926 would force any new liquid-cooled power plant either to be the paragon of all engines or to leave the field. The apparent reason for the Rolls-Royce advance was the nearly simultaneous application of an entire set of new techniques just coming to fruition at the time. To this may be coupled the unceasing efforts of one of the country's finest engineering teams that had become exhilarated by the knowledge that it was on to something out of the ordinary. The first of the new techniques was the reintroduction of the now-reliable reduction gear and the increase in crankshaft speed that it made possible. Both the engine and its propeller could run at optimum speed.

By the end of 1928 the gear-driven centrifugal supercharger, at last perfected by Ellor, had reached the manufacturing stage and was incorporated in the F-XI engine under two versions: MS for moderate supercharging at low altitudes, and S for full supercharging at high altitude. In addition, the supercharger was now beginning to be used at lower altitudes for getting more of the explosive mixture into the cylinders and thus adding another boost in power. By 1929 the supercharged F-XI was giving a maximum power of 620 bhp at 2,700 rpm, a speed with which even the Reed propeller could not cope.

At the same time, high-temperature and evaporative cooling were being investigated, as was the ram effect produced by the air entering at high velocity into the carburetor intake and adding a supplementary pressure to that produced by the compressor. A necessary complement now was the practical use of high-octane fuels, which were beginning to appear in quantity at the end of the 1920s after nearly ten years of

FIGURE 46.—Rolls-Royce Kestrel, 450 hp, 1932, powering a Fairey Fox II.
(Smithsonian photo A4667C.)

research. All of these improvements could be used to their full extent only with liquid-cooling, which added to these advantages an in-line construction of very low frontal area. Air-cooled engines, on the other hand, always would be forced to turn their cylinders squarely against the wind for successful operation at high power.

In 1930, when the F-XI engine was named the Kestrel, more improvements in design brought the introduction of some versions in which the maximum rotational speed was further increased to 3,000 rpm; and about 1933, after the adoption of salt-cooled exhaust valves, maximum power reached 750 bhp. Against such progress, the air-cooled radial engine was unable to keep pace, and it was soon realized that there was no alternative but to reintroduce liquid-cooled engines for fighter planes, for the first time since the Hispano-powered S.E.–5.

Specification 20/27 was then modified to accept liquid-cooled engines. Fairey had already developed the Firefly II fighter, which, with a fully supercharged Rolls-Royce F-XII engine, was able to reach 215 mph at 13,000 feet with a rate of climb of 2,200 ft/min. But Fairey was not given the chance to enter the high-performance field again, despite the hearty shove he had given aeronautical progress in 1925. No Fireflies

102

were ordered, at least not in Britain. When the export restrictions for his airplanes were lifted Fairey found an eager customer in the Belgian Air Force, from which important orders for Foxes and Fireflies were at last forthcoming. A Belgian Fairey Company was incorporated and a plant for the manufacture of Fairey airplanes was erected near Brussels. The beautiful Fairey biplanes remained the pride of the Belgian Air Force until they were replaced with Hawker Hurricanes just before World War II.

Another early effort to produce a fast fighter powered by a liquid-cooled engine was undertaken by the Westland Company. Westland built a high-wing fighter to take the Rolls-Royce engine, and it delivered the first such fighter to fly in Great Britain. This plane had a maximum speed of 188 mph, and it made a strong impression at the 1928 Hendon Display but never reached general production. Gloster tried to convert a Gnatsnapper model to carry the Rolls-Royce engine but its development did not progress past the prototype stage.

An opponent for the Hart finally came from Hawker itself when a low-drag Rolls-Royce-powered version of its F 20/27 prototype was built. This airplane, under the name Hornet, was one of the highlights of the 1929 Olympia Show in London. Later known as the Fury, this fighter entered service in 1931, but too late to claim its ascendency during the air exercises of that year; nevertheless, the Hart formations were successfully intercepted, this time by Demons, which simply were lightened two-seat fighter versions of the Hart.

The Hawker Fury, then, heralded the new era of the fast fighter in Great Britain, and from 1931 on the Rolls-Royce engine showed itself, with rapidly increasing evidence, in its true light—a fighter engine of formidable performance characterized by aluminum monoblock construction. This quality was to remain the hallmark of the type until the jet turbine, combining lighter weight with smaller frontal area and greater power, was to take over.

When making a comparative evaluation of the state of the art in 1928–1930, a period which was to be of much consequence for the evolution of the aircraft engine during the 1930s and up to World War II, we see an unfolding panorama.

America was achieving what it had set out to do. Thanks to the efforts of the Pratt & Whitney and the Wright firms, stimulated by the Navy, eight years of official and private research were crowned by the capture of a leading place in air-cooled engine development. Work on the Curtiss liquid-cooled engines slowed down and, for all practical purposes, was as good as halted after the Army declared that monoblock construction was not suited to high-temperature cooling, the only means, in their eyes, with which the liquid-cooled engine could still hope to outbid the achievements of an air-cooled engine. After 1929 the Army Air Corps also started buying pursuit planes powered with air-cooled engines, but perhaps not quite so wholeheartedly as the Navy.

In France, the Hispano-Suiza Company continued to build Hispano-Suizas, but these were no longer at the spearhead of progress and were better known for their reliability than for any new breakthrough in technology. Sensing the change of the tide, Hispano-Suiza had taken a license from Wright to build air-cooled Cyclones and Whirlwind types, reversing the pattern of 1916 that had led to the starting of the Wright Aeronautical Corporation as an aero engine manufacturing concern.

Italy also became completely committed to the air-cooled radial after 1930, and so did many small countries, some of which were content to apply for a license on the outstanding Bristol Jupiter engine.

The most decisive factor leading to the evolution of the aero engine was the air-cooled radial's complete takeover in commercial flying. The high-strung, liquid-cooled engine was not an interesting proposition as a commercial engine after 1930, but it would continue to be used extensively in fighter airplanes. With high power combined with small frontal area and with a reserve of still higher emergency power bursts for short periods of time (during which the liquid coolant could act effectively as a buffer against destructive overheating) this engine had no parallel for interceptors. As a power plant for high-speed fighter aircraft it had such ascendancy that it was again increasingly so used during the 1930s in spite of a greater vulnerability to bullet damage. But given the choice between performance and a possibly greater immunity when shot at, performance was preferred.

Britain had started research on the air-cooled engine, and for many years it had been the leader in its development. Paradoxically, after 1928 it was only in England that the liquid-cooled, in-line engine was pushed relentlessly—at first by Rolls-Royce only, although after 1931 a second wave of interest was already forming on a promise of still higher performance as a result of the extraordinary specific powers obtained in the highly specialized laboratory of H. R. (later Sir Harry) Ricardo. This development (which cannot be gone into here) was one that would bring the reciprocating internal combustion engine to the highest pitch of complicated wizardry—the Napier Sabre, a 24-cylinder, sleeve-valve engine.

The year 1928, the key year in aero engine progress, saw the introduction by Rolls Royce of an ambitious, large version of the F-X, with cylinders of 6-in. bore. The delicately nurtured monoblock construction was averse to big bores, and the H-X, as the engine was first known (later it would receive the name Buzzard), was not conspicuously successful. Nevertheless, it would gain its place in the hall of fame because it was the basis for the famous Rolls-Royce "R" engine, an all-out racing design producing 1,900 bhp in 1929 and over 2,300 bhp in 1931. It won for Great Britain the last two Schneider races—the final one being won without opposition—and the Schneider Trophy became the permanent possession of the Royal Aero Club.

The development of the "R" engine, which attained mean effective pressures and piston speeds beyond those reached by any internal combuston engine at that time, taught the Rolls-Royce engineers a great deal. It prompted them to undertake a design study for a new fighter engine based both on the "R" and on a steam-cooled Kestrel variant, named Goshawk, that was being developed as the intended successor of the Kestrel engine. The result of this latest design effort would earn immortality as the Merlin, which was to become the refined instrument of British air superiority during World War II. The development of the Merlin is a fascinating story that has been widely proclaimed.

The Rolls-Royce engineers had become struck by the same vision that had inspired Kirkham in 1917; and the whole K–12 evolution was, in a way, repeated. The first Merlin prototypes had their crankcases and water jackets cast in one piece, like the K–12, and though this construction should have benefited from 15 years of progress in aluminum casting, it had to be discarded again. Nor was a new form of cylinder head, on which great hopes had been built, giving satisfaction. The version that finally was successful as the Merlin II service engine was much more akin to the Kestrel, and thus to the F-X, than had been intended. Not until 1941 was a detachable cylinder head adopted with success. This is further proof that progress, when at the ceiling of specialized construction, does not come by leaps and bounds but by slow, intensive research leading to small but continuing improvements.

In America, meanwhile, the cause of the monoblock liquid-cooled engine had not been totally abandoned. Around 1928–1929, N. H. Gilman was manager of the Allison Engineering Company, a small firm that specialized in precision engineering and, for many years, in the building of special engines and parts for the Army and Navy under contract. Gilman became concerned with the situation of the D–12 and Conqueror engines confronting the Army specifications for high-temperature cooling. He decided to try his hand at a new design of monoblock construction that would be able to work at the high temperatures which the Army was determined to use in service.

At first, Gilman's design did not receive much encouragement, but when the Allison Company was taken over by General Motors in 1930 he was permitted to prepare a design for a 12-cylinder, liquid-cooled engine of 1,710 cubic inches swept volume and an intended 750 bhp, which was much more than any air-cooled engine was capable of at that time—the Hornet and Cyclone were rated at 575 hp. This design was started two years before that of the Merlin but it had nearly the same cylinder dimensions, the same length of stroke, and only a 0.1-in. greater bore. The designed power of 750 bhp was also the same as that originally laid out for the Merlin.

The Merlin was started in an already experienced plant and could with certainty count on all-out official support. Thus, Rolls-Royce could throw all of its available resources into the new project and at the same time be free to develop its engine as it best suited the engineering staff.

The V–1710 Allison had no such advantage and, although the future of that engine would testify to the soundness of its design, much time was needlessly lost. When first presented to the engineering division of the Army Air Force, the Allison was not even granted a hearing, first because the Army was still purchasing Curtiss Conquerors for its high-speed pursuit planes (Curtiss P–6s) and also because the Army engineers at Wright Field were then investigating new ideas for high-performance, liquid-cooled power plants. The only help the Army gave Gilman was its recommendation that he try his luck with the Navy.

The Navy, still fully committed to the air-cooled engine, was not very receptive at first, but on second thought its officials found that the V–1710 might be reworked into a reliable engine for the new dirigibles then being programmed. This decision would end the Navy's long dependence on a specialized German airship engine builder (Maybach). As a result, work was undertaken until about 1934 on the B model of the V–1710 engine, a fully reversible airship engine intended to give 650 hp at 2,200 rpm. This was as far removed from a fighter engine as could be imagined.

At the end of 1931 the Army at last awakened to the fact that its own high-performance design might take much more time than had been estimated, due to the inevitable slowness of any project for which every part has to be subcontracted by bureaucratic means. A new improved model of the V–1710 known as the C-type was then ordered, with the hope of quickly obtaining a 1,000-hp engine. The Army officials defeated their own purposes, however, by continually interfering with the engine's progress—trying to get too much too soon.

106

Apart from the exigency of a temperature of 300° F, work on a turbosupercharged version also was insisted upon, and still later a specification for fuel injection was added to the burdens of an already difficult development program. So, progress was delayed in spite of the fact that there had been no more doubts about the desirability of supporting liquid-cooled power plants after a standard P–36 airframe—normally powered by a Pratt & Whitney radial of latest design—was converted to receive the Allison engine. As the P–37, the maximum speed of this plane jumped from 300 to 340 mph. Following this demonstration, a new generation of fighters (the P–38, P–39, and P–40) was designed for and built around the Allison engine. These fighter planes came just in time to play a part in World War II.

Such examples of obstinacy with a fixed policy as the Army had shown in respect to the Allison are most often found among government bureaus. Even if fixed policies are conducive to technical progress, their importance is realized only after much loss of time. Private enterprise, on the other hand, has its own particular weakness when concerned with specialized research. Its managements are apt to become shy of a complicated research project at perhaps too early a stage because of a constant and—when left to their own resources—inevitable preoccupation with cost. The ideal is a close understanding between government and industry, but this, because of the corruption bugaboo, always has been a difficult goal to achieve.

The Rolls-Royce Merlin has been a shining example for the latter form of dynamic equilibrium. While the Allison's progress was being interfered with too much, the Merlin's was left free to be developed as it pleased Rolls-Royce, with the only official goal being "maximum performance." With no restriction on financial support, the development of the Merlin surged forward.

One of the profound early differences with the development of the Allison was that it was found wiser at Rolls-Royce to adapt the coolant temperature to the idiosyncrasies of the monoblock construction rather than try to force things the other way round. The coolant temperature for the Merlin thus was lowered to the maximum that the engine could stand, about 260° F. Finally, water again was used, and it was found to be the best cooling medium after all, in spite of its handicap—as one witty researcher remarked—of being too cheap.[6]

Nor was the development of the exhaust-driven turbosupercharger expedited in Britain. That development was to become an American achievement after 25 years of tenacious effort. The result was that the

---

[6] S. D. Heron, *History of the Aircraft Piston Engine*, 1961, page 92. Ethyl Corporation.

show on the Allied side was clearly stolen by the Merlin, which powered the Spitfires and Hurricanes that won the Battle of Britain. Later, it powered that 1941 realization of the philosophy that had led to the Fairey Fox: the De Haviland Mosquito, which was able to outfly any fighter extant by the use of every drag-saving device that was in the book, and some that were not. Last, but not least, American daylight bombing over Germany was saved, in part, by one of the happiest combinations that ever produced a fighter: the two-stage supercharged Merlin in the P–51 Mustang. Here, high speed and long range were exquisitely blended.

This long-range-giving quality of the liquid-cooled power plant was the result of a double advantage over the air-cooled engine. The first advantage was the higher efficiency of the engine itself, especially after the "high boost and low revs" technique was perfected. This technique could not be used to such an extent with air-cooling. The second advantage, obviously, was that a much lower frontal area permitted a lower powered and thus even a less-fuel-consuming engine to be installed for the same aircraft performance.

But the development of the air-cooled engine did not come to a stop. Superior designs were developed by Bristol, Wright, and Pratt & Whitney. The air-cooled engine for fighters was saved again, at the last moment, by the R–2800 Pratt & Whitney Double Wasp, at a time when the advisability of continuing the use of air-cooled engines on such aircraft was much in doubt.

The war in the Pacific was dominated by the air-cooled engine on either side, but the liquid-cooled monoblock engine, again by reason of superior efficiency and low drag, was able to execute some outstanding performances, most notable of which was the shooting down of Admiral Yamamoto by Allison-powered P–38 Lightnings that had flown to the limit of their range and with a timing that fully matched that of the Japanese Navy's supreme commander.

One of the possible advantages of the monoblock engine that definitely had been taken into consideration by the originator of the Hispano-Suiza in 1914 was that it might be mass-produced. Casting could be done quicker than the specialized welding that was necessary on the Mercedes-type engines. The difficulties encountered due to the need for high precision in the casting of the aluminum blocks defeated this purpose to a great extent during World War I, but these difficulties were overcome in World War II. Whereas production of the individual-cylinder Rolls-Royce engines in World War I could not be speeded up enough to satisfy the requirement of the armed services, the Merlin of World War II was made in quantities greater than could have been dreamed of before 1939.

In America, production of the Merlin was taken up by Packard (the one-time D–12 competitor) and great quantities were turned out. In October 1944, Dr. Nutt, as director of aircraft engineering and in charge of production at the Toledo plant, took up the work he had started with the D–12.

With the end of World War II, the days of the aluminum monoblock engine were numbered. A few attempts to adapt the Merlin to commercial aircraft remained inconclusive, and the air-cooled radial was left with the exclusive responsibility of powering the great airliners before transport and military aviation would switch over to jet propulsion.

Postwar racing saw, and still sees, the monoblock-engined Mustangs and Cobras stand up to racers powered by air-cooled engines of 28 cylinders despite two and a half times the swept volume and twice the power. In the former racers the value of low frontal area is shown again where reciprocating piston-engines are concerned.

So ends the development which the D–12 had started in 1922. No D–12 ever roared in anger. That engine was foreordained by Fate to be the peacetime American link between the French highlight in engine building of World War I and British supremacy in aero engines during World War II. America may well be proud of the achievement.

109

☆ U.S. GOVERNMENT PRINTING OFFICE: 1972 O—442-373

www.ingramcontent.com/pod-product-compliance
Lightning Source LLC
Chambersburg PA
CBHW060547100426
42742CB00013B/2486